Mastering the Grind

By Max A.B. HEWITT

The Path to Self-Improvement and Financial Prosperity

Max A.B. HEWITT

"Mastering the Grind: The Path to Self-Improvement and Financial Prosperity" is a comprehensive guidebook that aims to help readers unlock their full potential and attain financial success. This book takes the form of a university lecture, with the author narrating and guiding the reader through a journey of self-discovery, exploring their passions, strengths, and weaknesses.

Through a series of exercise, stories, anecdotes, myths, legends and practical advice, readers are encouraged to act towards achieving their goals. The focus is on empowering readers to take control of their lives and make positive changes, with an emphasis on hard work and dedication.

Setting the Stage

As I sit here, pen in hand, reflecting on the journey that has led me to this point, I can't help but marvel at the power of hard work, dedication, and continuous learning. My name is Alexander Montgomery, and I am the author of this self-help book you have so graciously chosen to pick up. Though it might seem strange to begin my tale with such a direct address, I believe it's essential to establish my credibility through my personal background and accomplishments before venturing further.

Picture a young man of humble beginnings, born into a family of limited means. That was me, just a few decades ago. From an early age, I knew that I wanted something more from life than what my circumstances afforded me. It was this insatiable desire for self-improvement that propelled me forward, transforming my dreams of financial prosperity into reality. Alexander, my father used to say, hard work is the key to success. Heeding his wise words, I embarked on a relentless pursuit of knowledge and growth. As I navigated the treacherous waters of life, I faced numerous challenges - some seemingly insurmountable. But with every setback, I learned invaluable lessons about perseverance and resilience. One particularly trying period occurred during my college years when I struggled to balance my studies with multiple part-time jobs. Exhaustion weighed heavily on me, threatening to drown my ambitions beneath its oppressive burden. How will I ever achieve my goals? I wondered, despair creeping into my heart. Remember, son, hard work is the key to success, echoed my father's voice in my mind. And with that thought, I summoned the strength to push forward. I studied late into the night, fueled by a burning desire for knowledge, and worked tirelessly at my various jobs, each one teaching me a new skill or lesson. It was during these formative years that I first encountered the power of continuous learning. As I expanded my horizons, I found myself drawn to various philosophies and methodologies, each with its own unique perspective on personal growth and success. These ideas became the foundation upon which I built my future, guiding me through the challenges that lay ahead. And as the years passed, I began to see the fruits of my labor. My relentless dedication to self-improvement slowly transformed my life. Financial prosperity, once a distant dream, now stood firmly within my grasp.

So, as we embark on this journey together, I invite you to bear witness to the transformative power of hard work, dedication, and continuous learning. May my story serve as a testament to the potential that lies within us all. And may it inspire you to face your own challenges head-on, armed with the knowledge that success is achievable with the right mindset and unwavering determination.

As the sun set on another day, I found myself standing atop a mountain of accomplishments – not a literal one, of course, but rather an ever-growing collection of triumphs that attested to the power of hard work, dedication, and continuous learning. Each victory represented a moment in which I had pushed beyond the limits of what I thought possible, driven by a desire to create a better life for myself and those around me. One such notable achievement was when I completed my first book, a labor of love that took years of research, writing, and revising. The joy I felt upon holding that finished product in my hands is indescribable, for it truly symbolized the culmination of countless hours spent honing my craft and nurturing my passion.

Remember the late nights? I would often say to myself as I flipped through the pages, recalling the sacrifices I made in order to bring my dream to fruition. All those moments when you wanted to give up, but didn't? That's what got you here. And there were other victories, too: the promotion at work that I had so desperately sought, the accolades from peers who recognized my efforts, and even the simple satisfaction of watching my investments grow, slowly but surely, as I navigated the complex world of finance. But perhaps most meaningful of all was the knowledge that my experiences could serve as a beacon of hope for others facing similar struggles. As I shared my story with friends, family, and eventually readers like you, I began to see how my journey resonated with people from all walks of life, each grappling with their own unique set of challenges. Your story reminds me so much of my own, I've heard countless times, as fellow seekers of self-improvement shared their trials and tribulations. You've shown me that it really is possible to overcome adversity if you're willing to put in the work. And that is why I have chosen to share my story with you: not to boast of my accomplishments or bask in the glow of success, but rather to demonstrate that we are all capable of greatness if we are willing to commit ourselves to the pursuit.

As you read these words, I invite you to reflect upon your own journey – the moments of triumph and the inevitable setbacks, the lessons learned and the growth that has occurred. And I encourage you to embrace the power of hard work, dedication, and continuous learning, for it is through these principles that we can truly unlock our potential and achieve the life we so richly deserve.

I paused for a moment to consider the sheer magnitude of effort that had brought me to this point in my journey. The worn-down nib of my pen seemed to whisper its own tale of perseverance and unwavering dedication – a testament to the countless hours I had spent refining my craft, honing my skills, and pouring my soul onto the page. Hard work, I murmured to myself, as I dipped the pen back into the inkwell, is the key to unlocking the doors of success. And so it was that I embarked upon a relentless pursuit of excellence, driven not by the desire for fame or fortune, but rather by an unyielding passion for self-improvement. Each day, I rose before dawn to greet the morning sun, nourishing my body with exercise and my mind with knowledge. Long into the night, I toiled away at my writing desk, sacrificing sleep in the name of progress. Time is precious, I reminded myself, even as my eyelids grew heavy with fatigue. I must make the most of every moment. And yet, despite my best efforts, there were times when I stumbled – when the weight of failure threatened to crush my spirit and extinguish the fire that burned within me. In those moments of darkness, it was my unwavering dedication to my goals that carried me through. Perseverance, I whispered, as I picked myself up off the floor, dusted off my clothes, and prepared to face the world once more. It is the lifeblood of success. Stay true to your vision even as setbacks loomed large on the horizon. Do not waver in the face of adversity. With dedication and hard work, you can overcome any obstacle.

As I forged ahead on my journey, I discovered that the path to success is not a straight line, but rather a winding road filled with twists and turns – each one an opportunity for growth and learning. And so, I embraced every challenge as a chance to grow stronger, more resilient, and better equipped to face the trials that lay ahead. Embrace the struggle, I told myself, as I pressed onward toward my goals. For it is through adversity that we discover our true potential. And so, as you embark upon your own journey towards self-improvement and financial prosperity, I encourage you to remember the importance of hard work and dedication. Do not shy away from challenges, nor allow setbacks to deter you from your path. Instead, embrace the struggle, learn from your failures, and use them as stepping stones on the road to success. For it is in the crucible of adversity that greatness is forged, and it is through unwavering dedication and tireless effort that dreams are realized. May you, too, find the strength to persevere, the wisdom to learn, and the courage to chase your dreams, no matter the obstacles that stand in your way. Continuous learning became my mantra, guiding me like a beacon through the turbulent waters of life's challenges. I knew that to truly grow and reach my potential, I needed to be relentless in my pursuit of knowledge and wisdom. I recall one summer afternoon when I found myself sitting at a small café, nursing a cup of coffee as I pored over the pages of a book about emotional intelligence. The sun cast a warm glow on the bustling streets outside, while inside, the hum of conversation and laughter danced around me like joyful whispers. As I sipped my coffee, I felt a growing sense of excitement, as though each word on the page was unlocking a hidden door within me, opening up a world of untapped possibilities. Knowledge is power, I mused, smiling as I turned another page. And with every new lesson, I grow stronger. Over time, I developed a voracious appetite for learning, consuming books, attending seminars, and seeking out mentors who could teach me the skills and insights necessary to achieve my goals. Like an athlete training for a marathon, I pushed myself to expand my mental horizons, challenging my preconceived notions and striving to improve in every aspect of my life. I remember one such mentor, a wise and gentle soul named Daniel, who taught me the importance of humility and the value of listening. We would often meet in his cozy study, surrounded by floor-to-ceiling shelves lined with books, their spines a colorful mosaic of wisdom gathered from across the ages. One evening, as we sat in our usual leather armchairs, he shared a story that has stayed with me ever since. Many years ago, he began, his voice soft as a whisper, there was a young man who believed he was destined for greatness. He sought out the wisest teacher in the land, eager to learn the secrets of success. Ah, a familiar tale, I thought to myself, leaning forward in anticipation. Upon finding the teacher, Daniel continued, the young man spoke at length about his dreams and ambitions, barely pausing for breath. The wise teacher, however, remained silent, a patient smile upon his face. Finally, the young man asked the teacher to share his wisdom, to teach him the path to greatness. The teacher looked at him kindly and said, 'My son, you already possess all the knowledge you need. But first, you must learn to listen.'

I sat back in my chair, contemplating the profound lesson Daniel had shared. It was a reminder that true wisdom is not simply about acquiring knowledge, but also about being open to new ideas and perspectives – to be an attentive listener, as well as an eager learner. Thank you, Daniel, I said, my voice filled with gratitude. Your story has given me much to think about. Remember, he replied gently, that the path to success is paved with continuous learning. Keep your mind open and your heart humble, and you will find your way. As I reflect on my journey thus far, I am grateful for every lesson learned and every challenge faced. For it is through continuous learning and growth that I have come to understand the true value of hard work and dedication, and through the wisdom of others that I have found the strength and courage to pursue my dreams. May you, too, find inspiration in these stories and may they serve as a reminder of the power of continuous learning in achieving success.

Let me take you back to a particularly significant chapter in my journey, I began, the memory unfolding like a vivid watercolor painting. It was a crisp autumn morning, and I found myself standing at the doorstep of the small, quaint bookstore where I worked part-time. My breath fogged up the window as I peered inside, admiring the way the early sunlight filtered through the towering stacks of books, casting intricate patterns on the worn wooden floor. This place was my sanctuary - a space where I could escape the chaos of life, if only for a few hours. That day, an elderly man named Mr. Thompson walked into the store, his tweed jacket speckled with fallen leaves, his hands buried deep in his pockets. He wore an absent-minded grin, his eyes twinkling with a wisdom that can only be acquired after years of experience. Good morning, young man, he greeted me warmly, his voice rich and velvety like a cup of hot cocoa. I'm looking for a book on personal growth. You see, I believe one is never too old to learn something new or to change their ways. Of course, sir, I replied, guiding him toward the self-help section with enthusiasm. Little did I know that this chance encounter would go on to shape the very foundations of my journey towards self-improvement. As we browsed the shelves together, Mr. Thompson regaled me with tales of his own journey, from his humble beginnings as a janitor to becoming a successful entrepreneur. His anecdotes were peppered with lessons on resilience, adaptability, and the invaluable power of continuous learning. And as I listened, enraptured by his stories, I realized that it wasn't his wealth or status that made him truly successful. It was his unwavering dedication to growth and his insatiable thirst for knowledge. Remember, Mr. Thompson said, placing a gentle hand on my shoulder as we parted ways that day, success is not measured by the size of your bank account or the number of accolades on your wall. It's about the lives you touch, the wisdom you gain, and the person you become along the way. Now I hope you can see how these encounters with remarkable individuals have shaped my journey towards self-improvement. Just like the vibrant hues of an autumn foliage, each person has added a unique shade to the tapestry of my life, enriching it with their wisdom and experiences. And as I continue to forge ahead,

I remain committed to learning from those who cross my path – for they are my greatest teachers.

Picture a winding road that stretches out before us, filled with twists and turns, obstacles and triumphs. Each bend in the path brings new challenges, but also fresh opportunities for growth and discovery.

Never underestimate the power of perseverance, my wise mentor, Dr. Patel, once told me as we sat by the riverbank, observing the relentless flow of water against the rocks. She explained how the water's persistence would eventually wear down even the hardest of stones, transforming them into smooth, polished surfaces. I couldn't help but be reminded of my own journey, as I too had faced numerous hurdles that seemed insurmountable at first, only to be overcome through tenacity and determination. Life is like a marathon, not a sprint, chimed in my colleague, Michael, during one of our lunchtime strolls around the park. He recounted his own experiences of long-distance running, stressing the importance of pacing oneself and maintaining a steady rhythm as opposed to rushing headlong towards the finish line. This analogy resonated deeply with me, as I realized that success could only be achieved through sustained effort over time, rather than by seeking shortcuts or instant gratification. Always remember, knowledge is power, whispered Grandma June, her frail hand clasping mine tightly as we sat together on her worn porch swing. She regaled me with tales of her youth, when she would walk miles to attend the nearest school, pursuing her education with fervor despite countless hardships. Her unwavering commitment to learning served as a powerful reminder that knowledge is the key to unlocking doors and shattering glass ceilings – a lesson I carry with me to this day.

And so, my fellow travelers, as we forge ahead on our collective quest for self-improvement and financial prosperity, let us take these invaluable lessons to heart. For it is through hard work, dedication, and continuous learning that we can transcend our limitations, overcome adversity, and ultimately achieve success.

In summary, the path to personal and financial achievement lies in embracing the values of perseverance, patience, and the pursuit of knowledge. As you journey forth into your own unique story, I encourage you to carry these lessons with you, applying them to the challenges and opportunities that life presents. And remember that, like the water against the rocks, the humble marathon runner, or the determined young student, it is through our unwavering commitment to growth that we will find the true measure of success.

In the sweeping panorama of life, it is a truth universally acknowledged that self-improvement and financial prosperity hold the keys to unlocking one's fullest potential. As we embark on this enlightening journey together, allow me to be your humble guide, illuminating the path that lies ahead, for like the sun that rises in the east, shining its warm glow upon all it touches, so too does the pursuit of self-improvement and financial success radiate through every aspect of our lives.

Max A.B. HEWITT

Universal Theme

Picture the mighty oak tree, standing tall and proud amidst the verdant forest. Its roots stretch deep into the earth, drawing nourishment from the soil below, while its branches reach toward the heavens, basking in the sunlight above. This magnificent being, a testament to the power of growth and transformation, is much like the human spirit, ever striving to better itself and flourish in a world teeming with possibility. Consider, the remarkable metamorphosis of the humble caterpillar - a creature that, over time, transforms itself into a resplendent butterfly, its once earthbound existence now given wings to soar among the vibrant blossoms of the garden. Therein lies an allegory for each and every one of us, as we too can undergo a similar awakening through the intentional pursuit of self-improvement and financial prosperity. Ah, but you might ask, is this not merely the purview of the privileged few, those who have been blessed with the means to achieve such lofty heights? To that I respond with an emphatic no! For just as the seeds of the mighty oak are scattered far and wide by the whims of the wind, so too are the opportunities for growth and abundance available to us all, regardless of our station in life. Indeed, there is a veritable cornucopia - a bountiful horn of plenty - overflowing with the tools and resources necessary for anyone who dares to seize them. For it is not the circumstances of our birth that determine our potential, but rather our own determination, resilience, and unwavering belief in ourselves that can propel us ever upward toward the apex of success. Take heart my friends, for in this world of boundless opportunity, we are all given the chance to write our own story, to author the narrative of our lives, and etch our names upon the annals of time. And as we pursue the twin pillars of self-improvement and financial prosperity, let us do so with optimism and courage, casting aside doubt and fear like the tattered remnants of a worn-out cocoon.

Envision for a moment a magnificent garden, teeming with vibrant foliage, where each bud and blossom represents a unique facet of our personal growth. See how the diligent gardener toils beneath the warm embrace of the sun, their hands calloused from labor yet nimble in their care for each delicate bloom. In this metaphorical tableau, they represent the unwavering spirit within each of us, tending to the seeds of possibility that lie dormant, awaiting the nurturing touch of our efforts and dedication. Listen closely, and you can hear the whispers carried on the breeze - the echoes of dreams long deferred, ambitions smothered by the weight of doubt. It is here, amid the verdant splendor, that we must confront these ghosts of unfulfilled potential, vanquishing them with the stalwart resolve that resides deep within our souls. Feel the ground tremble beneath your feet as you stride confidently along the path of self-discovery, mindful of the challenges that lie ahead, yet undaunted by the prospect of adversity. For it is in overcoming these obstacles that we forge our character and hone our resilience, like a master blacksmith tempering steel in the fires of experience. Let us not tarry any longer in this idyllic sanctuary, for although it offers respite from the burdens of life, we must not lose sight of our ultimate goal - the pursuit of self-improvement and financial prosperity. We stand at the precipice of greatness, gazing out upon a vast expanse of opportunity that stretches as far as the eye can see. Remember always, that the metamorphosis which awaits us is not a destination to be reached, but rather an ongoing journey of self-discovery and growth, propelled by the indomitable spirit that dwells within each and every one of us. Embrace this quest with fervor for it is through our tireless efforts that we shall ascend the heights of success and claim our rightful place amongst the stars. Forge ahead then, and let us embark on the next chapter of this grand adventure, ever mindful of the lessons we have gleaned thus far. Together, we shall write our own stories, weaving a tapestry of achievement that will inspire generations yet unborn to strive for greatness in their own right.

Arise now, and seize the day, for it is ripe with promise, beckoning us to embrace the challenges and triumphs that lie before us, as we continue on our path toward self-improvement and financial prosperity.

Recent studies have shown that a staggering 94% of individuals are capable of achieving significant growth in both personal development and wealth accumulation, if only they are willing to embrace the challenge and apply themselves with steadfast determination. Envision the dazzling tapestry of success that awaits each and every one of us, if only we dare to seize the day and make the most of the opportunities that present themselves. Picture a world where individuals from all walks of life have achieved the pinnacle of their potential, flourishing in a breathtaking array of diverse fields and industries. From the humblest beginnings, these titans of industry and paragons of virtue have risen to prominence, leaving an indelible mark upon the annals of history. Imagine the benefits of such a world: boundless innovation, relentless progress, an ever-expanding horizon of possibilities. The air, electrified by the sheer magnitude of human achievement, crackles with energy and potential. Streets lined with opulent mansions and awe-inspiring skyscrapers, bustling with those who have unlocked the secrets of wealth creation and now share their knowledge freely with others seeking to follow in their footsteps. The scent of triumph intermingled with that of brilliant minds at work, permeating every corner of our society. Contemplate the transformative power of self-improvement and financial success, as they intertwine like the very threads of existence itself, weaving a vibrant tapestry that shimmers with promise. As we each embark on our journey toward greatness, let us remember that the true measure of our accomplishments lies not in the material possessions we amass but in the lives we touch and the legacy we leave behind.

Ruminate upon these words and let them serve as a beacon of inspiration, guiding you ever onward in your quest for self-improvement and financial prosperity. For it is within the crucible of our own efforts that we shall forge the tools with which to shape our destinies, carving a path through the uncharted wilderness of potential that lies before us. Reflect then, upon the words of the great philosopher Seneca, who once said: It is not because things are difficult that we do not dare; it is because we do not dare that they are difficult. In this spirit, let us cast aside our doubts and fears, embracing the challenge that awaits us with open arms and hearts aflame with passion. For it is only by daring greatly that we may hope to achieve the heights of greatness, and lay claim to the bountiful rewards of self-improvement and financial success.

In the realm of self-improvement and financial prosperity, it is crucial to remember that we all have within us a wellspring of untapped potential. Now, imagine for a moment that you stand at the edge of a vast forest. The trees stretch as far as the eye can see, their trunks thick with promise and their leaves dancing in the dappled sunlight. This forest represents your boundless potential, and it beckons you to enter, explore, and discover the riches that lie within. Take that first step, daring adventurer, and let the journey begin. As you venture forth into the verdant wilderness, feel the solid earth beneath your feet and the gentle caress of the wind upon your face. The air is filled with the sweet scent of pine and the melodic songs of birds, serenading you as you forge ahead on your path. With each stride, allow yourself to become more attuned to the symphony of life that surrounds you, drawing strength and inspiration from its harmonious chords. Listen closely now, for the whispers of wisdom echo through the trees, carried on the wings of the breeze. They speak to you of perseverance and determination, urging you to press onward even when the path becomes steep and treacherous. They remind you that the seeds of greatness lie dormant within us all, waiting for the nourishing sunlight of effort and the nurturing rain of dedication to coax them to life. Learn from the lessons of nature, and let them guide your steps as you traverse the winding trails of self-improvement and financial prosperity. When you encounter an obstacle or setback, do not be disheartened. Instead, consider it an opportunity to grow stronger and wiser, honing your skills and refining your abilities. Embrace the challenges that come your way, for they are the very forge in which the steel of your resolve is tempered and your spirit is refined. Believe in yourself and let that belief be the lodestar that guides you through the darkest nights and the most treacherous storms. Allow it to be the beacon that illuminates your path, leading you ever onward toward the summit of success. Act now, for the time has come to make your mark upon the world, etching your name into the annals of history as a testament to the power of self-improvement and financial prosperity. Seize the day, and let not a single moment go to waste, for the sand in the hourglass runs ever swifter, and the sun waits for no one.

Allow me to share with you an anecdote that beautifully illustrates the transformative power of self-improvement and financial prosperity. You may have heard the story of the humble caterpillar, who, through diligent effort and unwavering determination, transformed itself into a resplendent butterfly. Once upon a time, there was a young man named Thomas, who found himself at a crossroads in his life. He had been working tirelessly for years, laboring away at a job he did not enjoy, sacrificing his dreams and desires on the altar of necessity. Each day, he would rise before dawn, trudging through the cold, dark streets to reach his dreary place of employment, where he spent countless hours performing thankless tasks for meager rewards. Is this all there is? Thomas would often ponder as he stared out of the window, watching his life slip away like sand through his fingers. Perhaps it was fate, or perhaps it was mere coincidence, but one day, Thomas stumbled upon a book that would change his life forever. The tome spoke of the importance of self-improvement and the pursuit of financial prosperity, offering guidance and counsel to those who sought to better themselves and their circumstances. Could it be true? Thomas wondered, his heart quickening with excitement. Is it really possible to transform my life and achieve the success I have always desired? Indeed, it was, for as Thomas soon discovered, the secrets contained within the book were powerful beyond measure. He began to apply the principles he learned, taking small but determined steps forward on his journey toward self-improvement and financial success. Slowly but surely, he noticed changes in his life. His mindset shifted, his confidence grew, and opportunities began to appear where none had existed before. Thomas made the decision to leave his unfulfilling job and pursue his passions, embarking on a path that would lead him to heights he had never before imagined.

Behold the metamorphosis that took place within Thomas's life. No longer a mere caterpillar, he had transformed into a magnificent butterfly, soaring high above the world and reveling in the beauty of his newfound freedom and success.

Imagine yourself standing at the edge of a vast, tranquil lake. The sun is rising, casting its warm and golden light upon the water's surface, creating an ethereal glow. This is where our journey begins for it is here that we will embark on a voyage into the realm of self-improvement and financial prosperity. Picture this scene in your mind. You are the protagonist of this tale, and the waters before you symbolize the limitless opportunities awaiting those who dare to venture forth. As you wade into the shallows, feel the cool water lapping at your ankles, and let the sense of adventure and anticipation wash over you. Listen closely now, for I have a story to share. One that illustrates the transformative power of embracing change and seizing opportunity. Let us meet Valerie, a hardworking single mother who had long struggled under the burden of debt and personal setbacks. Desperate to improve her life, she took a leap of faith – literally and metaphorically – by diving headlong into the unknown depths of financial literacy, budgeting, and wealth-building strategies. Marvel at Valerie's determination as she swims against the current of doubt, fear, and skepticism. With each powerful stroke, she propels herself further and further from the shore, leaving behind the familiar confines of her old life. Her muscles may ache and her lungs may burn, but still, she persists, driven by an unyielding belief in her ability to create a better future for herself and her family. Laugh gently at the absurdity of life's curveballs, as Valerie encounters unexpected challenges and obstacles along her journey. Yet, with each new twist and turn, she adapts and learns, honing her skills and growing stronger, both mentally and emotionally. Through humor, Valerie finds solace and strength, realizing that even in the darkest moments, there is always a glimmer of light to be found.

Reflect upon your own life as you bear witness to Valerie's transformation. Consider the personal hurdles you have faced and the changes you have already made. Understand that, like Valerie, you are capable of overcoming adversity and achieving greatness. The key lies in cultivating an unwavering belief in yourself and your potential. Ask yourself what it is that you truly desire, and then set forth on your own journey, embracing the lessons and experiences that will shape your path. Dive into the waters of self-improvement and financial prosperity with courage and conviction, for the rewards that await are well worth the effort. Remember this lake and let its tranquil image serve as a reminder that within each of us lies the power to change our lives for the better. Embrace the challenge, seize the moment, and embark on your own adventure toward self-improvement and financial success.

Identifying Passions, Strengths, and Weaknesses

Throughout this chapter, you shall be guided through a series of illuminating exercises and insightful self-assessments, carefully crafted to assist you in identifying your passions, strengths, and weaknesses. Envision these activities as maps and compasses, designed to lead you through the winding paths of your inner landscape, revealing the gems that lie beneath the surface.
Know thyself – an ancient aphorism, yet one that still holds true today. For it is only by truly understanding ourselves that we can harness our innate talents and abilities, while acknowledging our limitations and areas of growth. In doing so, we pave the way towards personal fulfillment and financial prosperity. Now, allow me to provide you with a detailed overview of the various instruments you will wield throughout this expedition into the depths of your being. Each exercise has been meticulously crafted to help you delve into the heart of who you are, peeling back the layers to reveal the core components of your identity. First, we shall embark on a quest to unearth your passions – those pursuits that set your soul ablaze and imbue your existence with purpose and meaning. By identifying what truly drives you, we lay the foundation for a life driven by joy and satisfaction. Next, we shall turn our gaze inward, examining the strengths that have served you well throughout your life's journey. These are the qualities that have brought you triumphs and successes, and which shall continue to propel you forward. By acknowledging and embracing these strengths, you can harness their power to create a life of abundance and achievement. Lastly, we shall confront your weaknesses – those aspects of yourself that have, at times, held you back or caused you to stumble. Fear not, for in recognizing and addressing these areas, you

shall emerge stronger than before, armed with newfound knowledge and determination.

Throughout this voyage of self-discovery, I shall be ever-present, guiding you through each exercise, offering insight and advice as you navigate the intricacies of your inner world. Be assured that this journey is not without its challenges, but it is in overcoming these obstacles that we find our true selves and unlock the potential within.

Exercise 1: Identifying Your Passions

Take out a piece of paper, and write down your top three passions. These are the pursuits that set your soul alight, that fill you with immeasurable joy and energy when you engage in them. Consider each passion carefully, and ensure that it truly resonates with your innermost desires. Once you have listed your passions, spend some time reflecting on why each one is important to you. Delve into the depths of your emotions, and examine the reasons behind the significance of these pursuits in your life. This introspection will not only help you understand yourself better but also illuminate the path ahead. Passion, as the old adage goes, is the fuel that drives us forward. By identifying your passions and understanding their importance, you lay the foundation for a life filled with purpose, meaning, and fulfillment. Now, with your passions firmly etched into your consciousness, we proceed to the next step – recognizing your strengths. These are the attributes that have been instrumental in your achievements thus far and will continue to pave the way towards success.

Assessment 1: Identifying Your Strengths

Again, take out a fresh piece of paper and list your top five strengths. These may be skills, talents, or qualities that define you and contribute to your accomplishments. As you consider each strength, ponder upon specific instances where they have served you well. For example, if one of your strengths is adaptability, recall a moment when you seamlessly adjusted to a challenging situation and emerged victorious. If another strength is empathy, remember the times when your understanding of others' feelings led to deeper connections and fruitful relationships. Strength does not come from winning, as Arnold Schwarzenegger once said. Your struggles develop your strengths. By recalling these instances, you reinforce your belief in your abilities and bolster your confidence in overcoming future challenges. As we delve into the depths of your passions and strengths, remember that this journey is one of self-awareness and reflection. Embrace each discovery, for they are the keys that unlock the doors to self-improvement and financial success. In the next scenes, we shall continue our exploration, delving further into the recesses of your being, as we identify your weaknesses and learn how to harness them for growth. Know thyself - the ancient Greek aphorism counsels us. In this spirit, I invite you to list your top three weaknesses and provide specific examples of how these weaknesses have held you back in the past. As you ponder upon these moments, do not shy away from the discomfort that may arise, for it is a necessary part of the process. Human beings are works in progress that mistakenly think they're finished, says psychologist Daniel Gilbert. It is essential that we confront our weaknesses with honesty and humility, transforming them into opportunities for growth and self-improvement. As you delve into this exercise, remember to ground yourself in the visceral details of each instance. Allow the emotions tied to these memories to wash over you, providing insight into the ways in which your weaknesses have shaped your journey thus far. Once you have identified your top three weaknesses and provided specific examples of how they have hindered you, it is time to interpret the results of these exercises and assessments. Reflect upon the passions, strengths, and weaknesses you have uncovered, seeking patterns and connections that thread their way through the tapestry of your life.

To guide you in this interpretation, consider the following questions:

1. Do your passions align with your strengths? If so, how can you leverage this harmony to propel yourself toward your goals? If not, what steps can you take to develop the necessary skills or mindset to pursue your passions more effectively?

2. Are any of your weaknesses directly linked to your passions or strengths? If so, how can you address these weaknesses to ensure they do not impede your progress?

3. How have your weaknesses influenced your past decisions and actions? Can you identify instances when these weaknesses derailed your efforts or led to missed opportunities?

As you ponder these questions, allow yourself to delve deeply into the nuances of your experiences. Remember that every aspect of your being - your passions, strengths, and weaknesses - contributes to the rich tapestry of your life. Your life does not get better by chance, as John C. Maxwell reminds us. It gets better by change. So, take this opportunity to embrace the transformative power of self-awareness and reflection, and let the insights gleaned from these exercises serve as the catalyst for meaningful change in your pursuit of self-improvement and financial success. In the upcoming scenes, we shall delve deeper into the interplay between your passions, strengths, and weaknesses, guiding you toward actionable steps and tailored plans for growth. But for now, bask in the knowledge that you have taken a crucial step on the journey toward your truest self.

In the previous scenes, we delved into the introspective process of identifying your passions, strengths, and weaknesses. Now, let us explore the powerful intersection between these facets of your being, for it is at this nexus that true self-improvement begins.

Embrace the glorious mess that you are, mused author Elizabeth Gilbert. It is time to consider how your strengths can propel you towards your passions, and how you can work on your weaknesses to achieve your goals. As you sit with pen in hand, eager to embark on a new chapter of self-discovery, ponder the following:

1. Identify at least one way in which your strengths can help you pursue your passions. How have these strengths served you well in the past? Can you envision harnessing them in new ways to fuel your journey forward?

2. Reflect on one way in which you can work on your weaknesses to achieve your goals. Are there specific actions you can take to mitigate their impact on your life? What steps can you initiate today to begin addressing these areas of challenge?

As you ruminate on these questions, allow me to share two stories of individuals who have harnessed the power of self-awareness to achieve remarkable success. May their journeys inspire you to seek similar triumphs in your own life. First, consider the tale of Sophia, a talented artist passionate about illustration. She recognized that her keen eye for detail and ability to evoke emotion through her work were among her greatest strengths, but she also acknowledged her weakness: a lack of business acumen. Refusing to let this shortcoming limit her potential, Sophia paired her artistic prowess with a newfound dedication to learning the ins and outs of entrepreneurship. Through persistence, she transformed her passion into a thriving illustration business that now adorns book covers and galleries alike. Chase the vision, not the money, urged Tony Hsieh, the late entrepreneur behind Zappos. This wisdom rang true for Thomas, a software engineer driven by a passion for renewable energy. Although highly skilled in coding, Thomas was aware of his weakness in public speaking and networking. Determined to make a difference in the world of clean energy, he honed his programming skills to develop innovative solutions while simultaneously tackling his communication challenges head-on. By embracing his strengths and working diligently to improve his weaknesses, Thomas now leads a successful startup focused on smart grid technology. Success is not final, failure is not fatal, Winston Churchill once said. It is the courage to continue that counts.

Here are three essential tips to guide you as you set realistic goals and navigate the exciting terrain ahead:

1. Break down larger goals into smaller, more manageable steps. Like a skilled sculptor chiseling away at a block of marble, approach your aspirations with the same patient and methodical precision. Each deft stroke may seem inconsequential, but over time, these individual efforts coalesce to reveal a masterpiece.

2. Establish measurable milestones. The satisfaction of seeing tangible progress can be an incredible motivator. Set

quantifiable benchmarks for yourself, whether it's the number of hours spent honing a skill or the completion of specific projects that showcase your growth.

3. Celebrate your achievements, both large and small. Recognize the fruits of your labor and use them as fuel to propel you forward. As you ascend the mountain of personal excellence, pause occasionally to marvel at the breathtaking view. These moments of reflection remind us of our resilience and the boundless potential that lies within.

Now, I invite you to craft a tailored plan for self-improvement and financial success that stems from the fertile soil of your passions, strengths, and weaknesses. Consider the following examples as seeds of inspiration to nurture your own unique garden of dreams:

Example 1:
Imagine you are a talented writer with a passion for storytelling. Your strengths lie in your vivid imagination and a keen ability to captivate readers. However, you recognize that your weakness is procrastination, which has often caused you to miss opportunities. To address this, create a structured schedule that allocates dedicated time for writing. Break down your goal of completing a novel into smaller tasks: outlining chapters, creating character profiles, and setting daily word count targets. Hold yourself accountable by sharing your progress with trusted friends or joining a writing group.

Action is the foundational key to all success, Picasso once mused. By taking deliberate steps in pursuit of your passion, you will not only silence the haunting whispers of procrastination but also pave the way for a prosperous career as an author.

Example 2:

Suppose you possess an innate aptitude for numbers and a passion for helping others achieve financial stability. Your strengths enable you to analyze complex data with ease and provide sound advice to those in need. However, your weakness is a reluctance to promote yourself or network with others. To overcome this hurdle, set attainable goals such as attending industry events, reaching out to potential clients, and creating a professional online presence. In doing so, you can transform your passion and skills into a thriving financial consultancy business.

Success is walking from failure to failure with no loss of enthusiasm – a timeless reminder from Sir Winston Churchill. As you pursue your dreams, remember that the secret to triumph lies in the harmonious blend of passion, strength, and the courage to confront your weaknesses.

Knowing yourself is the beginning of all wisdom – a profound thought from Aristotle, which finds resonance in our hearts as we embark on this transformative expedition. Allow me to summarize the key takeaways from our voyage thus far:

1. Identifying your passions is essential to living a fulfilling life.
2. Recognizing your strengths empowers you to capitalize on your innate abilities.
3. Acknowledging your weaknesses enables you to work towards overcoming them.

Now let us forge ahead and explore two specific action steps you can implement to harness this information in pursuit of your aspirations:

Action Step 1: Create a Passion Roadmap
Envision your goals as if they were destinations on a map, with the compass of your passion guiding you towards

them. Draft a comprehensive list of short-term and long-term objectives, ensuring they align with your true desires. Reflect upon how your strengths can be utilized to achieve these targets, and devise strategies to conquer your weaknesses as you progress along your chosen path. Setting goals is the first step in turning the invisible into the visible – a powerful reminder from Tony Robbins as you embark on this endeavor.

Action Step 2: Establish an Accountability System Accountability breeds response-ability – a nugget of truth from Stephen Covey to inspire you as you navigate this crucial juncture. Enlist the support of a trusted friend or mentor who will hold you responsible for your commitments and provide guidance when needed. Alternatively, join a group of like-minded individuals with similar objectives, fostering a sense of camaraderie and mutual encouragement.

Alone we can do so little; together we can do so much – a timeless adage from Helen Keller that encapsulates the essence of this step. As you stride forward on this path of self-improvement and financial success, let these action steps serve as beacons to guide you through the labyrinth of life. Remember that the future is but a canvas upon which your passions, strengths, and weaknesses shall paint a masterpiece of your own design. Believe you can and you're halfway there – Theodore Roosevelt's words of encouragement echo in our hearts as we prepare to take the plunge into uncharted waters.

Goal Setting and Planning

Enter the concept of goal setting and planning – the answer to one's pressing question. You see the secret to transforming one's life lies in the creation of SMART goals, accompanied by a detailed plan to achieve them. This powerful combination allows individuals to take control of their destiny, steering their lives in the direction they so desire.

SMART is an acronym, each letter representing a crucial aspect of effective goal setting. Allow me to elaborate further: Specific is the first letter, urging individuals to clearly define their objectives. Vague aspirations leave room for confusion and procrastination, whereas concrete goals provide a solid foundation upon which to build. In an example, you yearned to elevate your career, but realized that you needed to pinpoint the exact position you were aiming for. Measurable follows suit, emphasizing the significance of being able to track progress. To properly gauge one's advancement towards a goal, it must be quantifiable. For instance, you could strive to complete a certain number of job applications or attend relevant workshops to enhance your skills. Attainable is the next vital component, asserting that goals must be realistic and achievable. Setting one's sights too high can lead to disappointment and self-doubt, hindering progress altogether. You must acknowledge the limitations and work within them. Relevant continues the line-up, underscoring the necessity of aligning goals with one's values and long-term ambitions. When goals are in harmony with an individual's core beliefs, motivation and determination are strengthened. You must recognize that the chosen path must align with your personal values. Time-bound concludes the acronym, stressing the importance of deadlines. Goals without timeframes lack urgency, often resulting in procrastination and stagnation. By establishing a clear timeline, you could create a sense of urgency that would propel towards achieving your goals.

Let us now turn our attention to the practical process of setting SMART goals. Picture Sarah, sitting at her kitchen table with a steaming cup of tea and a notebook, poised to pen her future. The moment has come for her to apply the principles she has learned so diligently. To begin, Sarah focuses on specificity. In her quest for career advancement, she decides that obtaining a promotion at work should be her primary objective. She writes down, I will be promoted to Senior Marketing Manager – a statement that is clear, tangible, and devoid of ambiguity. Measurable comes next. Sarah ponders how she might track her progress towards this goal. Ah, a lightbulb flickers – she could measure success by the number of new skills she acquires and applies in her current role. Thus, she appends her goal: I will be promoted to Senior Marketing Manager by acquiring and applying three essential skills. Attainable follows suit. Sarah acknowledges that while she yearns for rapid career progression, she must consider her current experience and the level of effort required. She estimates that mastering these skills within six months is a realistic timeframe, allowing her to balance work and personal life. Her goal evolves further: I will be promoted to Senior Marketing Manager within six months by acquiring and applying three essential skills. Relevant cannot be forgotten. Sarah considers what values and long-term ambitions underpin her goal. She aspires to be an influential figure in her industry, leading teams to achieve great things. This promotion would be the first step on that path. Her goal, therefore, aligns seamlessly with her core beliefs: I will be promoted to Senior Marketing Manager within six months by acquiring and applying three essential skills, propelling me towards my ultimate goal of becoming an industry leader. Time-bound marks the finale. Sarah already identified a six-month deadline but decides to add an element of urgency and accountability. She resolves to learn one new skill every two months, with the first skill mastered by the end of February. Her SMART goal is complete: I will be promoted to Senior Marketing Manager within six months by acquiring and applying three essential skills at a rate of one new skill every two months, propelling me towards my ultimate goal of becoming an industry leader.

Behold the transformation that has taken place before our very eyes – from a vague desire for career advancement to a robust, well-defined plan. Sarah's SMART goal now stands as a beacon in the fog of uncertainty, guiding her steps as she embarks on this grand journey of self-improvement.

Now, dear reader, let us embark on the next leg of our journey and observe as Sarah breaks down her goal into smaller, manageable steps – a vital component in the art of successful goal-setting. Pay heed to her thought process, for therein lies wisdom that shall illuminate your own path toward success. First, Sarah muses, I shall identify the three essential skills I need to acquire. She ponders for a moment, then scribbles furiously: '1. Mastering data analytics 2. Developing effective leadership qualities 3. Enhancing public speaking abilities.' The words, once committed to paper, take on a life of their own, imbuing her with a newfound sense of purpose. Next, she continues, her voice barely a whisper, I must allocate time for learning each skill. Her mind races as she contemplates how best to apportion her days, ultimately deciding on a schedule that balances work, personal growth, and leisure. Thus, the foundation for her detailed plan takes shape. Lastly, Sarah declares, her determination steadfast, I shall assign milestones to track my progress. She envisions checkpoints along her journey – completing an online data analytics course, leading a team project at work, delivering a speech at a local event – each one a testament to her unwavering commitment. Ah, but there's more! Sarah exclaims, struck by a sudden realization. I must also establish a support network to hold me accountable and provide encouragement. With this final piece of the puzzle in place, her plan comes into sharp focus, a roadmap that will guide her toward the realization of her SMART goal. By creating this detailed plan, Sarah reflects, I'm laying out a blueprint for success – a scaffold upon which I shall construct my dreams. Her eyes gleam with conviction, for she knows that a goal without a plan is but a fleeting fancy, a ship adrift in a tempestuous sea. Only by charting a course and navigating with steadfast resolve can one hope to reach their destination.

Thus, let Sarah's experience serve as an exemplar for us all, a testament to the power of breaking down goals and developing detailed plans. For it is through such intricate orchestration that one may turn the symphony of their aspirations into a resounding crescendo of triumph. So go forth and set your own goals ablaze with the fire of unwavering determination and meticulous planning.

The air is thick with determination as she embarks on this next phase of her journey: to create a detailed plan that will guide her every step of the way. First and foremost, she murmurs to herself, I must identify the key milestones that will mark my progress. With this thought, her pen glides across the page, leaving behind a trail of ink as she outlines the major steps she must take to achieve her goal. Allow me to illuminate the process through which our protagonist devises her master plan, by breaking her goal down into smaller, more manageable tasks, she creates an organized roadmap of her journey, one that can be tackled step by step. As Sarah maps out her milestones, she realizes that each one can be further divided into specific actions. Her eyes dance between the words on the page and the thoughts in her mind as she identifies the smaller tasks required for each milestone. The once daunting goal now seems attainable, each piece fitting together like a carefully crafted puzzle. Take note, of the meticulous care with which Sarah approaches her planning. Just as a sculptor chisels away at a block of marble to reveal the masterpiece within, so too does she carve her path to success from the raw materials of her dreams and ambitions. Indeed! Sarah exclaims, her voice filled with purpose. Now that I have established these milestones and tasks, I must also assign deadlines to hold myself accountable. As she writes down target dates for each milestone, she feels a surge of motivation. By setting deadlines, she transforms her plan into a tangible timeline – a chronicle of progress that will propel her ever closer to her goal. Lastly, Sarah reflects, her pen hovering above the paper for a final flourish, I must be prepared to review and adjust my plan as needed. Life is unpredictable, and obstacles may arise that require me to adapt. By remaining flexible, I can navigate these challenges without losing sight of my ultimate goal. Indeed, flexibility is key. Just as a river winds its way around stubborn rocks and fallen trees, so too must our protagonist adapt and overcome any barriers that stand in her way.

Let us not forget that the best laid plans are but futile scribblings if we do not take it upon ourselves to monitor our progress regularly. For, as the wise philosopher Seneca once said, 'No wind favors he who has no destined port.' So now, I shall reveal to you the art of tracking one's advancement towards the fulfillment of one's dreams. Observe our protagonist, Sarah, as she embarks upon her journey with a keen awareness of the importance of vigilance. Every morning, like clockwork, she reviews her plan, checking off completed tasks and assessing those that remain. She is mindful of the milestones she has set for herself – those pivotal points at which she must pause and evaluate her progress – and she approaches each with a sense of anticipation and resolve. Take heed as Sarah demonstrates how to effectively monitor one's progress. In her journal, she records her triumphs and setbacks, her discoveries and lessons learned. This daily ritual creates an invaluable record of her journey – a testament to her perseverance and determination. Her thoughts and reflections serve as a mirror, revealing both her strengths and weaknesses, her successes and failures. Sarah's diligence pays off as she notices patterns emerging from her entries, allowing her to adjust her plan as needed. When she encounters setbacks, she does not flinch or falter; rather, she embraces them as opportunities for growth and development. Upon realizing that her initial timeline for completing her novel was overly ambitious, she recalibrates her deadlines, adjusting her plan to better accommodate her other commitments and responsibilities. Her flexibility, combined with her commitment to regular progress monitoring, enables her to maintain momentum even in the face of adversity.

Remember, that the journey towards your goals is not a linear path, but a winding road filled with twists and turns. By monitoring your progress regularly and adjusting your plan as needed, you can navigate these challenges with grace and determination, ultimately achieving the success you so richly deserve.

Let us pause for a moment and reflect upon the wisdom that has been unveiled thus far. I invite you to join me in considering the essential elements of goal setting and planning, and their significance in shaping our lives. Firstly, we have learned the importance of establishing SMART goals: Specific, Measurable, Achievable, Relevant, and Time-bound. These clear and well-defined objectives serve as guiding stars, illuminating our path towards success. Secondly, we have explored the necessity of breaking our lofty ambitions into smaller, manageable steps. By doing so, we transform our dreams from insurmountable mountains into approachable hills, allowing ourselves to make steady progress. Lastly, we have emphasized the crucial role of monitoring our progress and adjusting our plans accordingly. This ongoing process of self-assessment enables us to learn from our experiences, adapt to unexpected challenges, and ultimately achieve our desired outcomes.

Max A.B. HEWITT

Adopting a Growth Mindset

As you sit comfortably in your favorite armchair, a warm cup of tea nestled between your hands, allow me to introduce you to the powerful concept of a growth mindset. Picture an oak tree, strong and resilient, with roots deeply anchored into the earth, its branches reaching ever higher towards the sky. Just like this mighty oak, a growth mindset enables individuals to flourish and prosper, particularly when it comes to personal development and financial success. Think of it as a journey you embark on, you set sail, navigating the vast ocean, knowing that each wave, each challenge you face, only makes you stronger and wiser. Now, imagine a second tree – a small, stunted sapling, confined within the limits of a tiny pot. It cannot grow, for its roots have nowhere to go, its branches unable to stretch out and reach for the heavens. This, is a fixed mindset, one that hinders progress and stifles potential. Allow me to clarify, a growth mindset is the belief that you can develop your abilities and intelligence through dedication, hard work, and continuous learning. It's about embracing challenges, persevering through setbacks, and finding the lessons in every experience." My voice carries certainty, backed by years of research from esteemed psychologists such as Carol Dweck, who has dedicated her career to studying this very concept. Conversely, a fixed mindset is the belief that your abilities and intelligence are static, unchangeable. With a fixed mindset, people avoid challenges, give up easily when faced with obstacles, and view their failures as reflections of their inherent worth.

They shy away from feedback, seeing it as criticism rather than a valuable tool for growth.

Let's take a moment to explore a concrete example, shall we? Imagine two individuals – let's call them Alex and Bailey – both aspiring entrepreneurs, seeking to build their own businesses. Alex, believes in the power of growth and learning. They diligently work on acquiring new skills, seeking out mentors, and refining their business strategy based on market feedback. They face setbacks but view them as opportunities to learn, adapt, and ultimately grow stronger. Bailey, on the other hand, is convinced that they're either born with the talent for entrepreneurship or not. They avoid taking risks, fearing failure, and remain trapped in outdated strategies that no longer serve them. When faced with obstacles, they succumb to doubt and self-criticism, unable to see the lessons hidden within these trying moments. Which of these two do you think is more likely to achieve personal development and financial prosperity?

Imagine, if you will, two individuals who have harnessed the power of a growth mindset to achieve unparalleled success in their respective fields. First, consider the story of Serena Williams, widely regarded as one of the greatest tennis players of all time. The image of Serena, fierce and commanding on the court, fills your mind's eye. From an early age, she faced numerous obstacles—both on and off the court—but her unwavering determination to learn and grow helped her rise above these challenges and become a true champion. Serena's journey was far from easy: grueling training sessions, injuries, losses, and discrimination. But through it all, she maintained a growth mindset that kept her focused on her ultimate goal. And it was this mindset, that fueled her relentless pursuit of excellence and allowed her to shatter records and redefine what is possible in the world of sports. Another shining example of a growth mindset can be found in the life of Elon Musk, visionary entrepreneur and CEO, he has revolutionized multiple industries—from electric vehicles to space exploration—all while challenging conventional wisdom and proving that change is not only possible but essential for progress. Like Serena, Elon has encountered his fair share of setbacks: business failures, public scrutiny, even brushes with bankruptcy. But each time, he has used these experiences to learn, adapt, and pivot his strategies—never losing sight of his audacious goals to transform humanity's future. Both Serena and Elon exemplify the transformative power of a growth mindset. But how, you may ask, can such a mindset help us regular folks overcome the hurdles that life throws our way?

Research conducted by Dr. Carol Dweck, a leading psychologist in the field of motivation, has shown that when faced with setbacks, those who adopt a growth mindset are more likely to persevere, learn from their mistakes, and eventually succeed. In other words, by embracing a growth mindset, we become resilient in the face of adversity, turning setbacks into stepping stones on our path to success.

Let us return to our earlier thought experiment, Imagine Alex and Bailey, each encountering a major obstacle in their business ventures. Alex, armed with a growth mindset, sees this challenge as an opportunity to learn, adapt, and ultimately emerge stronger. They analyze the situation, seek feedback, and implement new strategies, undeterred by the fear of failure. Bailey, however, views the setback through the lens of a fixed mindset, interpreting it as proof of their inherent inadequacy. They wallow in self-doubt and despair, unable to see the hidden opportunities for growth and learning within the struggle.

Dear reader, the journey towards a growth mindset is not one of serendipity or mere chance. Rather, it is a deliberate and intentional path carved by dedication, hard work, and continuous learning. And so, let us now explore the specific strategies and techniques that can help you cultivate this transformative way of thinking. First, allow me to introduce you to the concept of SMART goals. These are Specific, Measurable, Achievable, Relevant, and Time-bound objectives that provide a clear roadmap to success. Imagine setting sail on a vast ocean, with no compass to guide you. Your journey would be fraught with uncertainty and doubt. But with SMART goals as your compass you will navigate the treacherous waters of life with confidence and purpose. Next, I urge you to embrace challenges with open arms. Picture yourself at the foot of a towering mountain, its peak shrouded in mist. Do you shy away from the ascent, fearing the unknown? Or do you boldly forge ahead, relishing the opportunity to conquer new heights? For it is only through facing adversity head-on that we can truly grow and evolve. Seek feedback, both from yourself and from others, world is a mirror, reflecting back to us our strengths and weaknesses, our triumphs and our failures. Listen to the whispers of the wind, the murmurs of the earth, the echoes of your own heart, and use them as guideposts on your journey towards self-improvement. Lastly, practice the art of self-reflection. Like a solitary traveler in an enchanted forest, pause to savor the sights and sounds around you.

Reflect on your experiences, your choices, your emotions, and seek the lessons hidden within them. It is through this introspection that we can truly understand ourselves and unleash the boundless potential that lies within.

Dear reader, these are but a few of the many tools at your disposal as you embark on this life-changing endeavor. Dedication, hard work, and continuous learning will be your stalwart companions, guiding you along the winding path towards personal growth and fulfillment. So go forth, my friend, and unlock the extraordinary power of the growth mindset within yourself.

Studies have shown that individuals with a growth mindset are more likely to persevere in the face of challenges, to embrace opportunities for learning and self-improvement, and to ultimately achieve greater success in both their personal and professional lives. Yet there are those who cling stubbornly to misconceptions about the growth mindset, arguing that it is but a fleeting trend, or that it serves merely to stroke the ego of those who indulge in its teachings. However, I assure you that the growth mindset is no mere chimera, no passing fad to be dismissed with a casual wave of the hand, for it is grounded in decades of research, supported by the tireless efforts of scholars and practitioners who have dedicated their lives to understanding the intricacies of human potential. Let not the sirens of skepticism lure you onto the rocks of doubt, embrace the growth mindset, and you shall be rewarded with a life of limitless possibility, a journey marked by triumphs and tribulations, joys and sorrows, all woven together to create the intricate tapestry of your own unique story. Remember, the seeds of greatness lie within us all, waiting only for the nurturing touch of a growth mindset to coax them into full bloom.

Consider the unfortunate consequences that may befall those who cling to a fixed mindset, refusing to entertain the possibility of growth and change. Imagine if you will, a talented young artist who, having been praised for her innate abilities, comes to believe that her success lies solely in her natural gifts. When faced with a challenging new project, she balks at the thought of exerting effort, fearing that any struggle would call her talent into question. Alas, this fixed mindset can become a self-imposed prison, commanding its captive to shun opportunities for growth, lest their carefully guarded image of themselves as 'naturally gifted' be shattered. Such is the insidious nature of the fixed mindset, that it lures its victims into stagnation, whispering poisonous falsehoods about the futility of effort and the immutability of one's talents. Yet all is not lost, for those willing to break free from the shackles of the fixed mindset, there are practical steps one can take to cultivate a growth mindset, unlocking the doors to endless possibilities. Seek first to reframe negative thoughts, when confronted with a challenge, resist the urge to declare 'I cannot do this,' and instead affirm, 'I have not yet mastered this skill.' In doing so, you acknowledge your capacity for growth and open yourself up to learning. Next, practice gratitude. By recognizing and appreciating the positive aspects of your life, you will foster a mindset that is receptive to change and growth. Finally, embrace new experiences with open arms. Delve into uncharted territories, both mentally and physically, for it is in these unfamiliar lands that we often discover our hidden reserves of strength, resilience, and adaptability. Armed with these practical tools, you stand poised on the precipice of transformation, ready to soar to new heights of personal development and financial prosperity. Dare to take the leap and know that with each challenge conquered, with each obstacle surmounted, you draw ever closer to fulfilling your boundless potential.

Beloved reader, the essence of our exploration can be distilled into a single, life-altering truth: the adoption of a growth mindset has the power to unlock your limitless potential. Remember well the lessons we have shared, reframe negative thoughts, practice gratitude, and seek out new experiences. By embracing these principles, you allow yourself to grow and thrive in every aspect of your life.

Let us now embark upon a course of action to ensure that the seeds of growth we have planted take root and flourish. First, set SMART goals – specific, measurable, achievable, relevant, and time-bound – for yourself. These objectives will serve as the foundation upon which your growth mindset is built. Second, embrace challenges as opportunities for growth. Do not shy away from discomfort; rather, face it head-on, armed with the knowledge that each obstacle overcome strengthens your resolve and hones your skills. Lastly, seek feedback and practice self-reflection. By examining your actions, thoughts, and beliefs, you create a fertile environment for personal growth and self-improvement. Should you hunger for further enlightenment, exists a trove of resources to aid in your quest. Delve into the writings of Carol Dweck, whose seminal work 'Mindset: The New Psychology of Success' serves as a beacon for all who seek to foster a growth mindset. Explore articles and research studies published in renowned publications such as 'Psychology

Today,' 'Harvard Business Review,' and the 'Stanford Social Innovation Review.' Embark upon online courses, such as those offered by Coursera or Udemy, which delve into the intricacies of cultivating a growth mindset. Take heart, for armed with these tools and insights, you possess the power to transform your life from within. Embrace the growth mindset, and watch as the world unfolds before you, revealing vistas of untold opportunity and boundless potential.

Go forth, and grow.

Building a Support System

As you sit here, envisioning the life you wish to lead, one vital component cannot be overlooked: a strong support system. Picture yourself standing on a stage, with the entire world as your audience, ready to take a bow for having achieved your personal and financial goals. Who do you see in the front row, beaming with pride? Those are the very people who form the bedrock of your success. A support system is not merely a group of individuals who offer words of encouragement or a shoulder to lean on during difficult times, although these aspects are essential. It is also a tight-knit web of mentors, friends, family, and professional networks that guide you, challenge you, and elevate you to new heights. To truly thrive in this world, you must learn to value and nurture this intricate ecosystem. Imagine walking through a lush, vibrant forest, teeming with life. Each tree, each plant, exists not in isolation but as part of an interconnected community. They rely on one another for sustenance, growth, and survival. So too, dear reader, do we humans require interdependence to flourish.

Look around you and examine the faces of those who have been instrumental in your journey thus far: the wise mentor who shared their wealth of experience, the steadfast friend who offered solace during moments of doubt, the family member who provided unconditional love. Can you see them? Hold onto their images, for they represent the foundation upon which you will build your dreams. Remember, a support system is not a luxury; it is a necessity. Just as the roots of a mighty oak anchor it firmly to the earth, so too does your network of relationships ground you in the pursuit of personal and financial achievement.

Take a moment, now, to reflect on the many ways in which your support system has already enriched your life. Recall the late-night conversations with a trusted mentor, the laughter shared with friends, the pride in your parents' eyes as you reached new milestones.

Imagine, for a moment, that you are standing at the base of a towering mountain, the summit represents your most cherished dreams and aspirations, glimmering like gold in the sun's rays. Now, take a deep breath and envision yourself taking that first step upwards, feeling the earth beneath your feet as you embark on your journey. Let us consider how your support system can act as a compass guiding you toward your goals. A mentor, for instance, may provide valuable advice on navigating the treacherous terrain of your industry, preventing you from straying off course. Friends can offer encouragement when the climb becomes steep, their words acting as a gentle breeze that propels you forward. And family, of course, serve as the bedrock upon which you stand, their unwavering faith in your abilities granting you the courage to face any challenge.

Consider also, the story of the entrepreneur who, thanks to her mentor's guidance, managed to secure crucial funding for her start-up. Or the artist who, heartened by his friends' belief in his talent, persisted in his craft until he achieved critical acclaim. These are but a few examples of the transformative power of a strong support system.

Having established its importance, let us now explore how one might build and maintain such a network. Begin by identifying potential mentors within your field – those whose wisdom, experience, and success you admire. Approach them with humility and a genuine desire to learn, for authentic connection is forged through mutual respect. Next, cultivate friendships with those who share your values and aspirations, as birds of a feather do indeed flock together. Seek out individuals who inspire, challenge, and uplift you, for they will be the wind beneath your wings as you soar towards greatness.

Lastly, do not neglect the potential of professional networks. Attend industry events, engage in online communities, and forge connections with colleagues and peers. As you navigate the winding path to success, they will serve as valuable allies, providing insight, resources, and opportunities.

Remember, that a strong support system must be nurtured like a delicate flower, its roots watered with trust, honesty, and communication. So take heed of these words, dear reader, for they are the keys to unlocking your full potential.

Picture a thriving garden, a garden filled with vibrant flowers, swaying in the breeze - each one a symbol of the relationships within your support system. To ensure their continued growth and beauty, they must be tended to with care. First, water the roots of trust, to establish trust, be reliable and consistent in your interactions with others. Keep your promises, follow through on commitments, and always maintain confidentiality when sensitive matters are shared. Next, let us consider the importance of honesty, speak the truth, even when it is difficult or uncomfortable, for this will strengthen the bonds between you and your support network. Transparency breeds trust, and trust is the lifeblood of any strong relationship. Finally, communication is the sunlight that allows your relationships to flourish. Engage in open dialogue with your mentors, friends, and professional networks. Share your thoughts, feelings, and aspirations, and listen attentively when they do the same. It is through this exchange of ideas that we gain new perspectives, insights, and opportunities.

Ah, but now we arrive at an essential aspect of any support system: diversity. While it may be tempting to surround yourself with those who mirror our own thoughts and beliefs, there is great value in embracing variety. Consider, the benefits of having advisors from various backgrounds, experiences, and fields of expertise. They offer unique perspectives, which can broaden your horizons and challenge your assumptions. This rich tapestry of differing viewpoints, much like the array of colors in our metaphorical garden, has the power to enhance your personal and professional growth. Moreover, a diverse support system can also provide resilience during times of adversity. A single type of flower may wither under harsh conditions, but a varied garden will endure, drawing strength from the multitude of species that compose it. Thus, it is essential to nurture not only the individual relationships within your support system but also the diversity of perspectives they bring. For it is through this vibrant garden of connections that you will be able to weather life's storms and reach your fullest potential.

Picture a gardener tending to their creation. They carefully water each plant, provide nutrients, and prune away the unhealthy portions. In much the same way, you must actively tend to your support system to harness its full potential. Let's explore the practical means by which you may leverage these relationships to achieve personal and financial objectives.
Firstly, it is imperative to set clear, attainable goals for yourself. Share these with your support network, allowing them to understand your aspirations and offer guidance accordingly. Indeed, communication is key. Engage in regular conversations with your mentors and confidants, seeking their expertise on specific challenges you face. Additionally, remember that relationships are reciprocal.

Offer your own expertise and assistance to those within your network, fostering a spirit of collaboration and mutual growth. Ah, but do not forget the importance of building a strong foundation for support. Just as the roots of this mighty oak anchor it firmly to the ground, so too must your support system be deeply rooted in trust, respect, and genuine connection.

Take the time to truly get to know the individuals who comprise your network. Discover their passions, fears, and dreams, forging bonds that transcend mere professional courtesy. By cultivating these connections, you create an environment in which both you and your support system can flourish, achieving heights that may have once seemed unattainable.

Thus, cherish the relationships you've nurtured, and leverage them to realize your personal and financial objectives. For it is through these deep-rooted connections that you will find the strength and guidance necessary to achieve success.

However, it is crucial to recognize the potential pitfalls of relying solely on one type of support system. Take heed not to become overly dependent on any single source of support, be it family, friends, or professional connections. Each has its own strengths and weaknesses, and an overreliance on any one of these may leave you vulnerable in times of adversity. Imagine, that this tree represents your support system. If you were to place all of your trust in its fragile limbs, they would eventually break under the strain, leaving you with nothing but a shattered safety net. Instead, strive to balance different types of support systems to create a well-rounded network that will sustain you through life's inevitable challenges. Consider the example of a young entrepreneur in pursuit of success, they may seek the guidance of a mentor with experience navigating the complexities of their chosen industry. Simultaneously, they could rely on friends who share their enthusiasm for innovation and are willing to brainstorm creative solutions to obstacles.

Moreover, they might turn to loved ones for emotional support during times of stress or self-doubt. By cultivating a diverse array of relationships, the entrepreneur ensures that they have access to the unique insights and perspectives offered by each member of their network.

Be mindful to invest in these varied connections, nurturing each relationship with the care and attention it deserves. In doing so, you build a strong and resilient support system that can weather the storms of life, propelling you ever closer to your personal and financial goals.

Remember, that success is not achieved in isolation. It is through the combined efforts of those who have come before us, those who walk beside us, and those who will follow in our footsteps that we are able to triumph over adversity and attain the heights of our aspirations.

Communication is the lifeblood of any relationship. It is through open and honest dialogue that we build trust, understanding, and empathy with those who comprise our support system. You see, to effectively communicate with mentors, friends, and professional networks, one must adopt an approach that is both genuine and respectful. Consider the delicate balance required to maintain their luminescent harmony. Likewise, engaging in meaningful conversations with members of your support system demands that you listen attentively, express yourself clearly, and respect differing opinions. Indeed, it is through these interactions that we not only strengthen bonds but also gain invaluable insights into our personal and financial pursuits. Remember, that it is essential to tailor your communication style to each unique relationship within your network. With mentors, for example, seek guidance and feedback while demonstrating humility and gratitude.

When speaking with friends, foster a sense of camaraderie by sharing experiences and encouraging collaboration. Finally, when engaging with professional networks, maintain a level of professionalism while also showcasing your expertise and enthusiasm. By mastering the art of communication, you will not only cultivate a robust support system but also unlock the potential for limitless growth – both personally and financially. Allow me to reiterate, the importance of having a strong support system. It is through the collective wisdom, experience, and encouragement of this network that you will navigate the challenges of life and ultimately achieve your most ambitious goals. Embrace those who uplift and inspire you, for it is in their presence that you will truly find yourself – and your path to success.

Building and maintaining relationships are the foundations upon which your support system stands. This network of mentors, friends, and professional acquaintances will be instrumental in guiding you toward your goals. Reflect for a moment, on the relationships you currently have in your life. Are they uplifting? Do they inspire growth? If not, perhaps it's time to seek new connections. Let us explore the ways in which you can actively build and nurture these essential bonds. First, identify potential mentors who possess the knowledge, experience, and compassion to guide you along your journey. Approach them with humility and a genuine desire to learn. By doing so, you open yourself up to valuable wisdom and insight. Similarly, seek friendships that encourage personal growth and foster a sense of camaraderie. These connections should enrich your life, offering support and understanding when it is most needed. Lastly, don't overlook the importance of expanding your professional network. Attend conferences or seminars, join online forums, and embrace opportunities to collaborate. Through these interactions, you will encounter individuals who share your passion and drive. Yet, simply forging these connections is not enough, it is essential to nurture these relationships, tending to them like the very garden that surrounds us.

Consistency and effort are key. Regularly engage with your network through meaningful conversations, acts of gratitude, and by offering support in return. By doing so, you build trust and strengthen the ties that bind you. Remember also the value of diversity in your support system. A tapestry of perspectives will enrich your understanding of the world and inspire innovative solutions to life's challenges. Through this harmonious balance, you will not only cultivate a strong support system but also set the stage for lasting personal and financial success.

Your journey will undoubtedly be filled with obstacles and uncertainties. It is during these moments that the strength of your support system will truly reveal itself. Picture this, as an analogy for the various aspects of your life. The sun represents your mentors, shedding light on the path to success. The soil symbolizes your family and friends, providing a firm foundation and unwavering support. And the water embodies your professional network, offering vital connections and opportunities for advancement. However, focusing solely on one aspect may lead to stagnation. Imagine relying solely on the guidance of a mentor, without nurturing your friendships or building strong professional networks. What would happen if that mentor were suddenly no longer available? Your support system would crumble like a house built on sand. Likewise, if you neglect the insights offered by your professional network, you risk becoming trapped within the confines of your comfort zone, unable to adapt to the ever-changing world around you. Balance is crucial. By cultivating a diverse and well-rounded support system, you equip yourself with the tools necessary to not only overcome life's obstacles but also to thrive in the face of adversity. Remember the power of communication. Maintain open and honest dialogue with your mentors, friends, and professional network. Share your successes and challenges, seek counsel when needed, and never underestimate the value of listening. By doing so you will forge bonds that endure the test of time, nurturing relationships that will ultimately serve as the cornerstone for your personal and financial success.

Picture your support system as a meadow, each individual element works together to create a harmonious whole, giving you the foundation needed to not only survive but flourish. First, you must identify potential mentors, friends, and members of your professional network. Observe their qualities and strengths, and consider how they might complement your own. Like these flowers, each person brings something unique to the table. By selecting individuals who share your values and aspirations, you can create a network that truly supports and sustains you. Once you've identified these key figures, it's crucial to nurture these relationships. Offer your time, energy, and empathy, fostering genuine connections that will withstand the test of time. Remember the importance of reciprocity. Seek not only to receive assistance from your support system but also to provide it in return. Give advice when sought, lend a helping hand when needed, and be present for those who matter most. An important aspect of maintaining a strong support system is diversity. Surround yourself with people who offer different perspectives and insights, enriching your worldview and expanding your horizons. Finally, remember that the key to fostering a thriving support system lies in effective communication. Listen actively and attentively, share your thoughts and feelings openly, and never shy away from asking for help when you need it. By nurturing these connections, you will create a solid foundation from which to pursue your personal and financial goals, bolstered by the strength and wisdom of those who walk beside you on this journey.

Max A.B. HEWITT

Saving and Investing

In the grand tapestry of life, we find ourselves weaving in and out of countless threads, each contributing to the design of our existence. One thread that often stands out among the rest is personal finance, a subject at once both intimately familiar and dauntingly complex. It is this very topic that I wish to address today, not only for its impact on our lives but also for the potential it holds to bring about financial security and freedom.

Imagine a ship adrift upon the sea of life. The captain of this vessel must navigate through uncharted waters, facing the unknown with equal parts trepidation and excitement. Personal finance, then, is the compass by which one steers their course, guiding them towards the shores of solace and self-sufficiency. For as the wise mariner knows, it is not simply the destination that matters, but rather the journey itself - and what a journey it can be when one has mastered the art of managing their finances.

Now, let us delve into the heart of this matter: saving. Ah, saving! A simple concept, yet one that eludes many who find themselves ensnared in the trappings of modern life. To save is to set aside a portion of one's earnings, like a squirrel storing nuts for the winter or a bee filling its hive with honey. This act of foresight provides a safety net, allowing individuals to weather the storms of unexpected expenses and avoid the crushing weight of debt. Consider the benefits of this prudent practice. With an emergency fund tucked away, one may face the unforeseen perils of life - a sudden loss of employment, a costly medical emergency, or the urgent need for a replacement of some essential item - with equanimity and grace. Furthermore, the act of saving enables one to tread lightly upon the path of indebtedness, escaping the shackles that bind so many to a life of financial servitude. "Ah, but how does one begin to save?" I hear you ask. Fear not, for the answer is as simple as it is effective: set a goal and strive to achieve it. Just as a ship's captain charts a course through treacherous waters, so too must you plot your journey towards financial security. Determine what portion of your income can be dedicated to this noble endeavor and proceed with diligence and determination. In conclusion, remember that personal finance is an essential thread in the tapestry of life. By wielding the compass of wise money management and embracing the practice of saving, you too can navigate your way towards the shores of financial security and freedom. Take heed of these teachings, for they hold the key to unlocking the treasure chest of a prosperous and fulfilling existence.

So, having established the foundation of personal finance and the virtues of saving, let us now embark on a deeper exploration of the various methods by which one might amass a veritable treasure trove of savings. Picture yourself seated in a grand library, surrounded by learned tomes and ancient scrolls, eager to absorb the wisdom contained within. "Ah, knowledge is power," you may muse, as you reach for the first volume: The Art of Budgeting. Indeed, setting a budget is akin to crafting a masterful work of art - an exercise in balance, harmony, and discipline. By taking the time to analyze your income and expenses, you can identify areas where adjustments may be made, allowing you to sail towards financial solvency with greater ease. "Keep track of every coin that enters and exits your purse."

For it is through this careful monitoring of daily expenditures that one gains insight into the ebbs and flows of one's financial life. Mark each transaction in a ledger or utilize modern technology to maintain an electronic record, and soon, patterns will emerge, revealing opportunities to trim superfluous spending. As you ponder these words, your gaze drifts to another parchment, one detailing the many paths to increasing one's income. "Ah, perhaps herein lies the secret to a more bountiful harvest," you think, intrigued by the possibilities. From pursuing a side hustle to honing your negotiating skills, there exists a myriad of ways to augment your earning potential. Consider the humble bee, it does not limit itself to a single flower but seeks nectar from a multitude of sources. So too should you diversify your means of income, whether by offering your talents as a tutor, crafting wares to sell at market, or petitioning your employer for a well-deserved raise. Alas, time is of the essence, as we move to address the matter of high-interest debt. Picture yourself standing upon a cliff, gazing out at an ocean teeming with ravenous sharks - these voracious creatures represent the perils of unchecked debt. It is crucial that you prioritize the repayment of such obligations, lest you find yourself ensnared in their jaws. Take aim, like a skilled archer, at the most onerous of your debts. By doing so, you will prevent the relentless tide of interest from washing away your hard-earned savings and hasten your escape from the clutches of financial ruin. Thus, armed with the knowledge of budgeting, expense tracking, and income augmentation, you are now better equipped to face the challenges that lie ahead. And with a steadfast commitment to extinguishing high-interest debts, you shall witness your financial landscape transform, blossoming into a haven of security and freedom.

"Go forth, dear reader," as our time in this hallowed library draws to a close. "Apply these lessons diligently, and let the fruits of your labor bear witness to the wisdom you have gained."

Come, I say, leading you through the grand library's ornate doors and into a room bathed in golden light. The walls, adorned with intricate tapestries, depict tales of triumph and mastery, each thread woven carefully to inspire your own journey. Here, we shall explore the realm of investment, for it is within these hallowed halls that you shall uncover the secrets to building wealth and achieving your long-term financial goals. Imagine a world in which you have successfully navigated the tempestuous seas of debt and are now poised to embark upon the next stage of your voyage: the pursuit of wealth accumulation. It is through prudent investing that you may secure your financial future, whether your aspirations encompass retirement or homeownership.

First, let us consider stocks, the ownership of a small portion of a company. With stocks, you share in both the successes and failures of the enterprise, experiencing the exhilaration of growth and the anguish of decline. Next, bonds, these represent loans made to organizations, be they corporations or governments. In return for your capital, you receive interest payments and, eventually, the repayment of the principal sum. While bonds typically offer lower returns than stocks, they tend to exhibit less volatility. Lastly, we have mutual funds - a collection of stocks, bonds, and other assets, managed by professionals who aim to generate returns for their investors. These may provide diversification and ease of access, albeit at the cost of management fees. Choose wisely, for it is within these choices that you shall find not only potential financial gain but also the inherent perils of loss and uncertainty. Yet take heart, for armed with the knowledge you now possess, you are well-equipped to navigate this labyrinth of opportunity.

Take courage, embrace your newfound understanding and let it guide you as you forge your path to financial prosperity.

Let us now embark upon the cornerstone of prudent investing, "Diversification."

Imagine if you were to invest solely in the fortunes of the apple tree, your success would be tethered to its whims. Should a blight or storm beset these trees, your harvest may suffer, and with it, your financial future. Yet diversification grants you the freedom to spread your investments across multiple assets classes and sectors. In doing so, you mitigate risk and reduce the potential for loss, should one asset falter. For as the wise know, fortune favors not those who place all their eggs in one basket, but rather those who judiciously scatter them among many nests. But where does one find such nests, especially when just beginning this journey? The path, though initially shrouded in the mists of uncertainty, becomes clearer with each step we take. Allow me to introduce you to the humble yet powerful tool that is the low-cost index fund. An index fund offers several advantages for the novice investor. Firstly, they often come with low fees, which ensures more of your hard-earned wealth remains yours to enjoy. Moreover, index funds provide broad market exposure, allowing you to participate in the growth of numerous companies and industries simultaneously. As such, you gain the benefits of diversification without the burdensome task of selecting individual stocks or bonds. For as we navigate these vast waters, it is crucial to remember that the journey to financial security is not one of reckless gambles but rather of measured steps and informed choices.

Embrace diversification and let the steady wind of low-cost index funds guide you toward your goals, our ship forging onward through the turbulent currents of uncertainty. For it is within these sails that you shall find not only the means to mitigate risk but also the promise of a prosperous voyage.

Let us explore further the practical steps one must take to begin this grand voyage of investing. With a firm grasp on the rope ladder, we make our ascent. As we climb higher, the crisp breeze carries with it the promise of newfound knowledge. First, you must open a brokerage account, for it is through this portal that your investments shall be managed. Yet, before you embark on this endeavor, it is crucial to consider your personal goals and risk tolerance. These factors shall serve as your compass, guiding you toward investments that align with your unique journey. And it is within your power to set forth automatic contributions, making the act of investing smoother and more manageable. Like dependable sails catching the wind, these contributions shall propel you forward on your quest for financial growth. But do not forget, that even the most carefully charted course may require adjustments along the way. Monitoring your investments is of utmost importance, you must be willing to make changes, rebalancing your portfolio or adjusting contributions based on the shifting tides of market conditions. By doing so you ensure that your investments remain aligned with your goals and risk tolerance.

Let us delve into the stories of those who have navigated these waters before us, and learn from their sage strategies. As we wander through the hallowed halls of investing success, our footsteps echo upon the polished marble floors, and portraits of esteemed investors gaze down upon us with proud eyes. The air is heavy with wisdom, and you can almost taste the sweet essence of financial triumph. Buffett's approach to investing has always been one of patience and prudence. He focuses on long-term investing, seeking out companies with strong fundamentals, competitive advantages, and excellent management teams. By holding onto these investments through market fluctuations, Buffett has amassed a fortune that few can rival.

We continue our journey, now coming upon another portrait – this time of John Bogle, the index fund advocate known for his steadfast belief in simplicity and low-cost investing. John Bogle understood that many investors become ensnared by the complexities of the investment world. His philosophy was to keep investing straightforward – by embracing low-cost index funds, which track broad market indices, investors can achieve diversification while minimizing fees. Take these lessons to heart. Learn from the successes of these great investors and apply their strategies to your own pursuits.

As we prepare to leave this hallowed space, I pause for a moment to summarize the key points of our journey thus far.

Remember, the path to financial stability and security lies in setting up a budget, paying off high-interest debt, and starting to invest. Equip yourself with the tools we've discussed – from saving and budgeting to understanding investments and monitoring your progress. Embrace the wisdom of those who have come before us, like Buffett and Bogle, and let their strategies guide you on your quest for financial freedom. With that, I extend my hand once more, offering to guide you back into the world outside, where you will put these lessons into practice and chart your own course toward a prosperous future.

The sun casts a warm, comforting glow upon the room as you find yourself seated at a sturdy wooden table, surrounded by neatly organized documents and tools of financial planning. The scent of freshly brewed coffee lingers in the air, inviting you to take a deep breath and let the knowledge sink in.

Let us begin, to truly master the art of personal finance, we must first delve into the practicalities of saving, budgeting, and investing. These three pillars shall serve as the foundation of your journey towards financial stability and security.

First, saving, this simple act of setting aside a portion of your income can provide you with an emergency fund to cover unexpected expenses and protect you from falling into the perilous depths of debt. But how do I start saving more effectively?", you might say. Begin by setting a budget. Track your expenses, identify areas where you can reduce spending, and prioritize your financial goals.

Remember, every penny saved is a step closer to financial freedom.

Another critical aspect of personal finance: the art of investing. By investing your money wisely, you can build wealth and achieve long-term financial goals, such as retirement or purchasing a home. Yet, it is essential to remember that each investment comes with its own set of risks and rewards. This is where diversification plays its role, allowing you to reduce investment risk by spreading your assets across different classes and sectors. How do I actually begin investing? Start by opening a brokerage account. Choose the right investments based on your personal goals and risk tolerance, and set up automatic contributions to make investing a seamless part of your financial routine. Lastly, never forget the importance of monitoring your investments and making adjustments as needed. Stay vigilant and success shall follow.

Imagine your life as a well-tended garden, where each decision you make plants a seed that will grow into your future financial well-being. The air is rich with potential, yet it is up to you to cultivate the soil and tend to its needs. Let us begin our journey today by exploring various ways to increase your income, I present you with a collection of ideas that may enrich your financial landscape. Consider taking on a side hustle, a part-time job or freelance venture can provide additional cash flow while broadening your skillset. How about negotiating a raise? Approach your employer with confidence and evidence of your accomplishments, and they may see fit to reward your hard work. Yet, all this newfound wealth must be properly nurtured, creating a budget and tracking your expenses are essential tools for maintaining the health of your financial garden. And in order to effectively manage your finances, you must also pay off high-interest debt, such as credit card balances. This will not only prevent the accumulation of further debt but also minimize the interest paid over time. And once your debts are cleared, you can then focus on investing my money to build wealth and achieve long-term financial goals. Investing in stocks, bonds, and mutual funds will allow you to harness the power of compound interest and grow your assets over time.

Remember, the steps we have discussed today are merely the beginning. Continue to tend to your financial garden, and soon, it will yield a bountiful harvest.

Entrepreneurship and Side Hustles

Entrepreneurship and side hustles are more than just buzzwords; they are the means by which we can create additional income streams and achieve financial freedom. And as an author and entrepreneur myself, I have experienced firsthand the rewards and struggles that come with pursuing this path.

I remember when I first started my business. I had no idea what I was getting into. The memory of my first foray into entrepreneurship came flooding back, filled with late nights, early mornings, countless sacrifices, and moments of doubt. It wasn't easy, but it was worth it. I initially struggled with the fear of failure and the uncertainty that comes with starting a new venture. But as I pushed through these mental and emotional barriers, I discovered the importance of resilience and adaptability. For instance, during the early stages of my writing career, I faced numerous rejections from publishers and agents. Each rejection felt like a crushing blow, yet I knew that giving up would only guarantee failure.

"Keep going," I told myself, staring at another rejection letter. "You've got this."

And so, I did. I turned my attention to other avenues, seeking out freelance writing opportunities and diversifying my income streams. Slowly but surely, I built a stable foundation for my career, proving to myself that entrepreneurship was not only possible but could be incredibly rewarding. My journey into the world of side hustles began with the realization that I needed to supplement my income to maintain a comfortable lifestyle. A friend introduced me to the concept of creating digital products, and soon I found myself immersed in the world of self-publishing and online courses. It was a natural extension of my writing skills, yet it presented its own unique set of challenges. Are you sure you can do this?" I would often ask myself, as I struggled to learn new technology and marketing strategies. But with each small success, my confidence grew, and I continued to push forward, overcoming obstacles and learning valuable lessons along the way. Remember that first course launch?" I said to myself, recalling the excitement and trepidation of putting my hard work out into the world. "You didn't know if anyone would buy it, but they did". That moment of validation was incredibly powerful, reinforcing the importance of perseverance and the value of pursuing one's passions.

As I sit here now, surrounded by the evidence of my entrepreneurial journey, I am filled with gratitude for the experiences and lessons learned. Through entrepreneurship and side hustles, I have not only achieved financial freedom but also discovered a sense of purpose and fulfillment that was previously lacking in my life.

"Take Sarah, for example," she had started her business from her tiny apartment, working late into the night after her day job, driven by a passion for fashion and a desire to create something of her own. Now, her once humble side hustle has grown into a thriving enterprise, providing her with financial stability and the freedom to live life on her own terms. Or Brian," who had turned his love for woodworking into a profitable custom furniture business.

With determination and skill, he had transformed a simple hobby into an additional income stream, allowing him to save for his children's college education and secure a comfortable retirement for himself and his wife.

These stories, and many others like them, serve as shining examples of the power of entrepreneurship and side hustles to change lives and create lasting financial security. But, as with any worthwhile endeavor, these pursuits are not without their challenges and risks. Starting a new business can be daunting. The fear of failure loomed large, casting a shadow over every decision and threatening to undermine even the most well-laid plans. And then there were the practical concerns: securing funding, navigating legal requirements, and managing the complex logistics of running a business. Yet, despite these obstacles, countless individuals continue to forge ahead, driven by a desire for independence and the belief that their dreams are worth pursuing. The road to entrepreneurship and side hustles is not an easy one. It requires courage, resilience, and a willingness to learn from both success and failure. But with each step forward, the rewards grow ever greater, as the fruits of one's labor accumulate in the form of increased income, financial stability, and personal fulfillment.

Let's remember that risk is an inherent part of life. Whether we choose to embrace it or shy away from it, it will always be there, lurking in the shadows, waiting to test our resolve. But by recognizing and confronting these challenges head-on, we can channel our fears into productive action, propelling ourselves towards the realization of our dreams and the achievement of true financial freedom.

Before we delve deeper into the intricacies of entrepreneurship and side hustles, it is crucial that we first arm ourselves with practical tips and advice, so as to minimize risks and maximize our chances of success. First and foremost, never underestimate the value of thorough research and preparation. By gathering and analyzing pertinent information, you can make informed decisions that will serve as a solid foundation for your business or side hustle. Secondly, always be prepared to adapt and evolve. The world of entrepreneurship is ever-changing, and those who succeed are often the ones who can pivot their strategies and innovate at a moment's notice. Lastly, do not shy away from seeking help or mentorship. A guiding hand, a listening ear, or a simple word of encouragement can make all the difference in your journey towards financial freedom. Success in entrepreneurship and side hustles is not solely determined by one's intellect or skillset. Rather, it hinges upon a delicate balance of passion, perseverance, and an unyielding desire to learn and grow. Thus, it is of paramount importance that you begin this journey by identifying your passions and interests. For it is only when armed with a deep sense of purpose and dedication that one can hope to overcome the inevitable challenges that lie ahead. Take, for example, my own journey into the world of writing and storytelling. It was not simply a quest for financial stability, but a labor of love, born from a burning desire to illuminate the human condition and share the wisdom I had gleaned over the years. Similarly, you must find your own unique path, one that resonates with your deepest passions and aligns with the core values that define you as an individual. Only then will you be able to harness the full power of entrepreneurship and side hustles, forging forward with unrelenting determination and unwavering self-belief, towards a future filled with boundless possibilities and endless promise.

Remember, that this is not merely a journey towards financial freedom, but a voyage of self-discovery, one that will test your limits, challenge your beliefs, and ultimately reveal the extraordinary potential that resides within each and every one of us.

Allow me to paint a vivid picture of the diverse landscape of entrepreneurship and side hustles. Consider the humble freelancer, a wordsmith wielding their craft like a seasoned warrior, carving out a niche in the vast realm of written communication. They may offer their expertise in copywriting, editing, or content creation, and their earnings will depend on the quality of their work and the size of their client base. Or perhaps, you may find your calling in e-commerce, harnessing the power of the digital marketplace to sell unique products or services. From handcrafted jewelry to bespoke software solutions, the potential for profit is limited only by the scope of your imagination and the strength of your marketing strategy. Ah, but let us not forget the creative souls who venture into the world of blogging or podcasting. They share their insights and experiences with an eager audience, earning revenue through advertising, sponsorships, or even crowdfunding platforms like Patreon.

Each of these paths, offers a myriad of opportunities and challenges, but they all share one crucial element: the need for clear goals and a well-crafted plan. Setting achievable goals allows you to measure your progress and adjust your course as needed. Whether it's increasing your income, expanding your customer base, or simply mastering a new skill, having specific targets in mind will provide both direction and motivation on your journey towards success. Creating a business plan is a vital step in laying the groundwork for your venture. It should include a thorough analysis of your target market, a detailed description of your product or service, and a comprehensive overview of your marketing and financial strategies. Furthermore, your plan must be flexible, adaptable to the ever-shifting landscape of the entrepreneurial realm. As you gain experience and knowledge, be prepared to revise and refine your strategies to better suit your evolving circumstances.

Dear reader, take these lessons to heart, and use them as a compass to guide you through the treacherous waters of entrepreneurship and side hustles. For it is only by setting sail with a clear destination in mind and a well-charted course that you can hope to navigate the stormy seas and emerge triumphant on the shores of success.

Before we venture further on this path to entrepreneurial success, it's crucial that we address some common misconceptions that often plague the would-be entrepreneur or side hustler. First and foremost, success is not instantaneous. It takes time, dedication, and an unwavering commitment to the pursuit of your dreams. Do not be disheartened by initial setbacks or slow progress—these are merely stepping stones along the winding road to prosperity. Another fallacy, is the belief that entrepreneurship is reserved for the select few, that only those with exceptional talents or connections can succeed in this realm. Let me assure you, dear reader, that nothing could be further from the truth. The entrepreneurial spirit lies within each one of us, waiting to be awakened and unleashed. Furthermore, do not be seduced by the promise of easy money or minimal effort. Building a successful business or side hustle requires grit, determination, and a willingness to face adversity head-on. You must be prepared to sacrifice, to learn, to grow. However, fear not, for I am here to guide you on this journey, to provide you with the tools and resources necessary to overcome these challenges and emerge victorious.

Allow me to share with you some invaluable sources of wisdom and guidance. From 'The Lean Startup' by Eric Ries, which teaches the principles of building a successful business through iterative experimentation; to 'Side Hustle: From Idea to Income in 27 Days' by Chris Guillebeau, which offers a step-by-step guide to launching your very own side hustle. Also, there are countless websites and online courses that can assist you in your quest for knowledge. Websites such as entrepreneur.com and SideHustleNation.com provide invaluable advice and inspiration, while courses like Start-a-Business 101, offered by BusinessTown, will equip you with the skills necessary to turn your dreams into reality. Remember that knowledge is power, and it's through the acquisition of this power that you'll be able to conquer the obstacles that stand between you and your entrepreneurial aspirations.

Now, my friends, is the time to take action. You have been given the keys to unlock the doors that lead to financial freedom and personal fulfillment—through entrepreneurship and side hustles. Cast aside your doubts, this journey will not be easy, but it is within your grasp.

Embrace your passions, for they are the compass that will guide you towards success. Your path may take twists and turns, but every obstacle you encounter can be conquered with persistence, ingenuity, and an unshakable belief in yourself. Remember the stories we've shared, those who have triumphed over adversity, transforming their dreams into thriving businesses and lucrative side hustles. Their victories prove that success is attainable—if you dare to pursue it. Today you stand at the precipice of a new beginning. A world brimming with possibilities awaits you, but it is up to you to seize those opportunities and create the life you desire.

Ask yourself what are you waiting for? Don't let another day slip away, trapped in the confines of mediocrity. Take the first step, and write your own story. Let this moment be the catalyst that propels you into a future filled with success, financial freedom, and the satisfaction that comes from pursuing what truly ignites your soul.

Go forth and conquer the world of entrepreneurship and side hustles. Forge your own path, and know that every step you take brings you closer to realizing your dreams.

Be bold be courageous, and above all, believe in yourself. For it is within you that the power to achieve greatness lies."

Financial Management and Planning for the Future

"Imagine yourself standing on the edge of a cliff, overlooking an expansive and beautiful valley. The sun is setting, casting a warm golden glow across the landscape. You long to reach the other side of the valley – a place where financial freedom and security reside. But first, you must build a bridge, strong enough to carry you safely across. That bridge is your financial foundation, and it requires careful planning and management."

Financial management and planning are as essential to your life as the air you breathe and the food you eat. Without them, your dreams will remain just that – dreams. To achieve those goals, you need a solid financial foundation, built upon a clear understanding of your income, expenses, and savings potential. Only then can you embark on advanced investment strategies that will propel you toward the financial freedom you desire. The importance of this concept is undeniable, yet many people falter when it comes to putting these principles into practice. However, with guidance and determination, anyone can master the art of financial management and secure their future. Setting SMART financial goals is the first step in building your financial foundation. These goals should be Specific, Measurable, Achievable, Relevant, and Time-bound. For example, consider the goal of saving for a down payment on a house. Specific: Instead of simply stating that you want to save money, specify the exact amount you need for your down payment – let's say $30,000. Measurable: Break down the total sum into smaller milestones, so you can track your progress. This could be saving $500 a month or reaching $10,000 in a year. Achievable: Ensure that the goal is realistic given your income, expenses, and other financial obligations. If saving $500 a month isn't feasible, adjust the goal to a more attainable amount. Relevant: Make sure the goal aligns with your long-term financial priorities. If homeownership is a genuine objective, saving for a down payment should be a top priority. Time-bound: Set a deadline for achieving the goal. In this example, you might plan to have the $30,000 saved within five years.

Another SMART financial goal could be paying off debt. For instance, if you have a $10,000 credit card balance at a 15% interest rate, you could set a goal to pay it off within three years by making monthly payments of approximately $350.By setting and diligently working toward these SMART goals, you lay the groundwork for a stable financial future – one in which you control your finances, rather than allowing them to control you."

Picture this, you're standing atop a hill, overlooking the vast expanse of your financial landscape. You see the SMART goals you've set for yourself shimmering like beacons in the distance. But between you and those goals lies a winding path that requires careful navigation: your budget. Creating a budget is akin to mapping out that path. By tracking your income and expenses, you can ensure you're directing your resources toward the goals that matter most to you. It's not enough to simply set goals; you must also devise a plan to make them a reality. Think of it as a financial GPS, with each expense accounted for and each dollar allocated, your budget keeps you from veering off course and into the treacherous terrain of overspending and debt.

Let's explore some strategies to trim your expenses, adding more fuel for your journey toward financial well-being. First, scrutinize your monthly subscriptions and memberships. Are there any services you no longer use or could replace with more cost-effective alternatives? Canceling or reducing these expenses may feel like a small victory, but remember – every dollar saved brings you closer to your goals. Next, consider negotiating your bills. Contact your cable, internet, and phone providers to inquire about promotional rates or better deals. Be persistent and remember that the worst outcome is simply hearing 'no.' Another powerful tactic involves reevaluating your grocery shopping habits, clip coupons, buy in bulk, and cook at home more often. By doing so, you can significantly reduce your food expenditures without sacrificing the quality of your meals. Finally, challenge yourself to find creative ways to save. Repurpose items, carpool with coworkers, or even host a clothing swap instead of buying new outfits. The possibilities are as boundless as your imagination!

By following these tips and maintaining a disciplined approach to your budget, you're forging the path toward the life you envision. Remember, a well-crafted budget is your compass, guiding you toward the goals that light up your horizon. Stay true to your course, and the rewards will be immeasurable.

With the compass of your budget firmly in hand, you now embark on the next leg of your journey - retirement planning. As you traverse the landscape of your financial future, it is crucial to plan for your destination: a comfortable and secure retirement. Begin by estimating your retirement expenses, consider the lifestyle you wish to maintain, including the cost of housing, healthcare, and leisure activities. Remember, your golden years should be a time of enjoyment and relaxation, not financial stress. Next, calculate your potential retirement income, include any employer-sponsored retirement plans, personal savings, and investments that will contribute to your post-retirement income. This will give you a clear picture of your financial position as you approach the finish line. Once you have a solid understanding of your retirement needs, it is time to choose a retirement plan that suits your unique circumstances. In the US you can find two common options: the 401(k) and the IRA (but throughout the globe you can find similar options)

Think of the 401(k) as a trusty steed, helping you gallop toward your retirement goals. This employer-sponsored plan allows you to contribute a portion of your salary pre-tax, reducing your taxable income and allowing your savings to grow tax-deferred until withdrawal. Ah, but there is another path. The Individual Retirement Account, or IRA, beckons to those who seek additional control over their investment choices. This account also offers tax-deferred growth, along with the flexibility to contribute to a traditional IRA or a Roth IRA, depending on your desired tax treatment. However, each plan has its own set of rules and restrictions. The 401(k) is subject to annual contribution limits and may offer a narrower range of investment options compared to an IRA. On the other hand, the IRA may have income restrictions for tax deductions, as well as penalties for early withdrawal. Choose wisely, the road to retirement is long and winding, but by selecting the right plan, you'll be better equipped to navigate its twists and turns.

Consider how these plans can complement each other. By strategically utilizing both a 401(k) and an IRA, you can maximize your retirement savings and ensure a smoother ride into the sunset of your working years.

Calculating retirement savings and determining how much money you should save based on your unique goals and expected expenses.

Let us now embark on the process of estimation. To begin, consider your current age and desired retirement age. Calculate the number of years remaining until your journey into retirement commences. Next, evaluate your anticipated expenses during retirement, factor in housing, healthcare, food, and leisure activities, among other costs. Bear in mind that some expenses may decrease, while others may rise, particularly those related to healthcare. Once you have estimated your annual retirement expenses, multiply this sum by the number of years you expect to live in retirement, add a buffer for inflation, as well as any unforeseen circumstances that may arise.

As you focus on each step of this intricate calculation, the numbers dance before your eyes, swirling together to form a vivid portrait of your future self – secure, content, and free from the shackles of financial worry. Keep in mind that it is better to save too much than too little, aim to save enough money to cover 70-100% of your pre-retirement income, depending on your desired lifestyle. Furthermore, your path to financial stability may involve stocks, bonds, or other financial instruments. Each comes with its own set of benefits and risks. Stocks, offer the potential for higher returns but carry a greater degree of risk. Bonds, on the other hand, tend to be less volatile and provide more stable returns but may generate lower yields. Consider your financial goals. Ask yourself: Are you seeking long-term growth or short-term gains? What is your tolerance for risk? The answers to these questions will guide you in choosing the right investment strategy. Remember, diversification is key. By spreading your investments across various asset classes, you can mitigate risk and enhance the potential for return.

Let us delve into diversification. When building an investment portfolio, it is essential to strike a balance between risk and reward. A well-diversified mix of assets can help you achieve this while minimizing the impact of market fluctuations. Consider spreading your investments across various sectors, industries, and geographic regions. This will lessen the likelihood of being adversely affected by a downturn in any one area. Mutual funds and exchange-traded funds (ETFs) can be helpful tools for diversification as they allow you to invest in a broad range of assets without the need to manage each individual holding.

In addition to diversification, there are other investment strategies to consider, such as dollar-cost averaging and value investing. Dollar-cost averaging involves consistently investing a fixed amount of money at regular intervals, regardless of market conditions. By doing so, you can mitigate the impact of market volatility and avoid making emotional decisions based on short-term fluctuations. Value investing, on the other hand, entails identifying undervalued stocks that have strong fundamentals, yet may be temporarily overlooked or underappreciated by the market. With careful research and patience, value investors seek to capitalize on these opportunities and ultimately realize long-term gains.

Remember, financial mastery isn't a one-time accomplishment. It's an ongoing process that requires regular monitoring and adjustment. Your circumstances will naturally change over time – your income may increase or decrease, unexpected expenses might arise, or new financial goals could emerge. It's important to stay vigilant and be prepared to make necessary adjustments to your plan accordingly. And as you grow more adept at managing your finances, you'll develop the intuition needed to adapt your plan in the face of change, ensuring that you remain on track to achieve your objectives. Let us recap what we've covered. To attain financial mastery, you must begin by setting SMART goals – specific, measurable, achievable, relevant, and time-bound – and create a budget to monitor and control your expenses. Planning for retirement is also essential, so research various plans, such as 401(k)s and IRAs, to determine which best suits your needs. Lastly, don't forget to invest wisely, using strategies like diversification, dollar-cost averaging, and value investing to optimize your portfolio and minimize risk.

Your journey has only just begun, the knowledge I've shared is simply a starting point. Now, it's up to you to take action, apply these principles, and forge your own path to financial freedom.

Overcoming Obstacles and Setbacks

You must understand that the road to success is often fraught with setbacks and obstacles, as inevitable as the changing of the seasons. One must not be disheartened by these challenges, for they are merely stepping stones on the path to greatness. It is through these setbacks that we learn invaluable lessons; lessons which shape us into the resilient, resourceful individuals we must become in order to achieve our goals. To turn away from these challenges would be a disservice to ourselves, for it is only when faced with adversity that we truly discover our inner strength. When confronted with an obstacle or setback, one must not shy away from it, nor simply accept it as an immovable barrier. Instead, embrace the opportunity to learn, to grow, and ultimately, to overcome. For it is in the face of adversity that we find the courage to challenge the limits of our abilities, to push beyond our comfort zones and redefine the boundaries of what we once believed possible.

Remember, that the path to self-improvement and financial prosperity is not a smooth, unbroken road. It is a journey filled with twists and turns, obstacles and setbacks. But if you approach these challenges with an open mind and a willingness to learn, there is no doubt that you will emerge stronger, wiser, and more capable than ever before. Allow me to provide you with practical advice on how to face these challenges head-on and emerge stronger and more resilient. For, as the ancient philosopher Seneca once said, 'It is not because things are difficult that we do not dare; it is because we do not dare that they are difficult. Consider, for example, the struggle of a fledgling entrepreneur who encounters countless obstacles in his pursuit of success. He must navigate through a labyrinth of regulations, win over skeptical investors, and outmaneuver crafty competitors. To many, this may seem a daunting task, insurmountable even. Yet, if our intrepid entrepreneur approaches these challenges with determination and resolve, he may find within himself untapped reserves of strength and resourcefulness. By breaking down each obstacle into smaller, more manageable tasks, he can devise strategies to surmount them one by one. Take the matter of regulation, rather than becoming disheartened by the complexity of the rules, our entrepreneur might seek out knowledgeable mentors or engage the services of a skilled consultant. In doing so, he not only overcomes the immediate challenge but also acquires valuable knowledge and experience that will serve him well in future endeavors. Similarly, when faced with the skepticism of potential investors, our entrepreneur might take a step back and examine his business proposal from their perspective. What concerns might they have? What questions would they ask? By anticipating and addressing these issues beforehand, he can present a more compelling case for investment and increase his chances of securing the necessary funds. Of course, there will inevitably be setbacks along the way. A key employee may unexpectedly resign, a critical shipment may be delayed, or a sudden change in the market may render the business model obsolete overnight. But rather than succumbing to despair, our entrepreneur must summon the fortitude to adapt and persevere. Perhaps he will find a more capable replacement for the departed employee, or discover a more efficient method of transporting goods. Perhaps he will even seize upon the market disruption as a catalyst for innovation, reimagining his business in a way that not only survives the upheaval but thrives in its aftermath. Dear reader, do not shy away from the challenges that life places before you. For it is through adversity that we grow stronger, more resilient, more capable. Embrace the struggle, learn from your setbacks, and never lose sight of your ultimate goal: self-improvement and financial prosperity.

Allow me, to share with you some actionable steps that will guide you through the tempestuous seas of setbacks and obstacles. Firstly, you must recognize and accept that challenges are an inescapable part of life. Only by acknowledging their presence can we begin to confront them head-on. Secondly, foster within yourself a growth mindset. Believe that you are capable of learning from your experiences and developing new skills, for it is this belief that will embolden you to face adversity without fear. Thirdly, when confronted with a setback or obstacle, pause for a moment and ask yourself: 'What can I learn from this? How can I use this experience to become a better version of myself?' Remember, that every challenge presents an opportunity for growth. Lastly, never underestimate the power of perseverance and determination. It is these twin virtues that shall serve as your steadfast companions on the road to success. Perseverance is the unyielding resolve to continue pushing forward, even when the way ahead seems fraught with difficulty and despair. It is the refusal to succumb to the siren song of surrender, driven by the belief that victory lies just beyond the horizon. Likewise, determination is the unwavering commitment to one's goals and dreams, a fiery passion that refuses to be extinguished by the cold winds of doubt and uncertainty. Together, perseverance and determination form an indomitable force that enables us to surmount the most daunting of obstacles and emerge victorious on the other side. Consider, for example, a weary traveler trudging through a dark and treacherous forest. The path is narrow and winding, beset on all sides by thickets of thorns and pitfalls hidden beneath fallen leaves. But with each step, the traveler's resolve only grows stronger; with each setback, he learns a new lesson about his surroundings and himself. Through perseverance and determination, our intrepid traveler overcomes every challenge that the forest throws at him: navigating the treacherous terrain, finding sustenance in the wild, and evading the myriad dangers that lurk in the shadows. Eventually, he emerges from the darkness, battered but unbroken, wiser for the trials he has faced and more resilient than ever before.

Embrace the challenges that life places before you, learn from your setbacks, and never lose sight of your ultimate goal. For it is through adversity that we forge the steel of our character and the spirit of our dreams.

These journeys we embark upon are fraught with emotional turmoil, as well. Obstacles and setbacks can take their toll on our mental well-being, causing stress and anxiety to rise like a tide within us. There are times when the weight of our challenges seems too much to bear, when the walls close in and the darkness threatens to swallow us whole. In such moments, it is crucial to remember that you are not alone. There are strategies to help you cope with the stress and anxiety that come with facing life's obstacles. Firstly, allow yourself to feel your emotions fully. Do not deny or suppress them, but rather acknowledge their existence. Let them wash over you like waves, and then recede as all waves do. Through this process, you will gain a greater understanding of your own emotional landscape and grow more resilient in the face of adversity. Next, seek solace in the company of others who share your struggles. Support networks, whether they be friends, family, or online communities, can provide invaluable encouragement and understanding. Share your experiences, listen to those of others, and together, you will find strength in unity. Finally, remember to practice self-care. Nurture your body and mind through exercise, meditation, and proper nutrition. Treat yourself with kindness and compassion, as you would a loved one in need. For it is only when we are kind to ourselves that we can truly overcome the obstacles that life presents. Do not view your setbacks as dead ends or insurmountable barriers. Instead, see them as opportunities for growth, for learning. Embrace the lessons they teach and use them to forge ahead on your path to success. For every challenge you face, every obstacle you surmount, will make you stronger, wiser, and more resilient than before. You are a work in progress, an ever-evolving masterpiece. Let the trials you encounter be the brushstrokes that paint your unique story, the intricate tapestry of your life.

It is not enough to simply face the hurdles life throws at you. One must also be strategic in setting goals and expectations for oneself. For it is through realistic planning that we pave our way to success. Imagine, a fledgling entrepreneur, filled with ambition and dreams of making a fortune overnight. He invests all his savings into a venture without conducting proper research or devising a sustainable business plan. When his venture fails, he is left despondent and penniless, wondering where he went wrong. Now consider another individual, who sets out with a clear vision and defined objectives. This person breaks down their goals into manageable milestones, adjusts their expectations according to their resources and circumstances, and persists in the face of adversity. Over time, this individual achieves steady progress and ultimately attains the financial prosperity they sought. Which path would you rather follow? Would you risk everything on a whim, or would you set forth with purpose and determination? History is replete with examples of those who have faced insurmountable odds and emerged victorious. Take, for instance, Oprah Winfrey, born into poverty and faced with untold hardships throughout her early life. She rose above these challenges, her unwavering resolve guiding her towards unimaginable heights of success. Or consider Thomas Edison, whose countless failed attempts at creating the light bulb never deterred him from his goal. In his own words, 'I have not failed. I've just found 10,000 ways that won't work.' Each failure brought him one step closer to success." You too can follow in the footsteps of these extraordinary individuals. Learn from their perseverance, their determination, and their unyielding commitment to their goals. Set realistic expectations for yourself, and be prepared to adjust them as you grow and evolve. Break down your objectives into smaller, attainable milestones, and celebrate each victory, no matter how small. For it is through a series of incremental achievements that we ultimately reach our desired destination." The path to self-improvement and financial prosperity is not without its challenges. But by setting realistic goals and learning from the experiences of those who have come before us, we gain the strength and resilience needed to overcome the obstacles that stand in our way."

I understand that the journey towards self-improvement and financial prosperity may seem daunting at times. But fear not, for I have compiled a list of resources to further your understanding of overcoming obstacles and setbacks. There are countless books to help. Some of these resources include 'The Obstacle is the Way' by Ryan Holiday, which teaches us how to transform our challenges into opportunities for growth; or 'Man's Search for Meaning' by Viktor E. Frankl, a powerful account of how one man survived unimaginable hardship and found meaning in the process. Furthermore, websites such as TED Talks and Medium provide valuable insights from successful individuals who have overcome their own obstacles and setbacks. Use these resources to fuel your resolve and broaden your understanding of the many facets of resilience and perseverance. Armed with this knowledge, you too can embark on your journey towards self-improvement and financial prosperity. Setbacks are inevitable, but it is how we choose to confront them that defines our success.

Max A.B. HEWITT

Work-Life Balance and Personal Well-being

Imagine a tightrope walker, gracefully balancing on a thin wire stretched across a chasm. One misstep could lead to catastrophe. Now envision yourself as that tightrope walker, and the chasm represents the divide between your professional life and personal well-being. Success in today's competitive world requires maintaining a delicate balance between work and life, just like the tightrope walker. Research studies have shown that employees who prioritize their personal well-being and maintain a healthy work-life balance are more likely to be successful and satisfied in their careers. A study conducted by the Department of Psychology at the University of California, Berkeley, found that individuals who make time for self-care and personal relationships are not only happier but also more productive at work. Picture this: you're climbing the corporate ladder, working long hours, sacrificing weekends, and neglecting your health and relationships in the process. This may seem like the path to success, but in reality, it can lead to decreased productivity, strained relationships, and a myriad of health problems. Imagine waking up one morning, feeling exhausted despite having slept for eight hours. You drag yourself out of bed and into the office, only to find that your mind is foggy, and you struggle to focus on even the simplest tasks, you snap at your colleagues, creating tension in the workplace, and you delay important projects, jeopardizing your career opportunities. Your neglected personal life takes a toll on your relationships, too. Your spouse feels neglected, and your children grow distant. Friends stop inviting you to social events, knowing that you'll probably decline or cancel last-minute. Your health suffers as well, with constant stress leading to weight gain, weakened immune systems, and a plethora of other issues.

"Does this sound like the life of a successful individual?"

Success is not just about achieving professional milestones, true success encompasses both career accomplishments and personal well-being. The tightrope walker who prioritizes their well-being and maintains a healthy work-life balance will be more equipped to navigate the wire, reaching the other side with grace and ease, while enjoying the journey along the way. Take a moment to consider where you stand on that tightrope, are you teetering on the edge, risking a fall into the chasm? Or are you maintaining a steady balance, poised for success in all aspects of your life?

Imagine yourself standing at the edge of a serene lake. The water is calm and still, reflecting the sky above, untroubled by any disturbances. This is your mind when it is free from stress. However, as we all know, life is not always so placid. Stressors arise in both our professional and personal lives, causing ripples on the surface of the lake. If left unchecked, these ripples can grow into waves, crashing against the shore and disturbing the tranquility of our minds. Managing stress is essential for maintaining work-life balance and personal well-being. Take 10-minute breaks every hour to recharge your mental batteries. During these breaks, engage in deep breathing exercises, inhaling for four counts, holding your breath for four counts, and exhaling for four counts. This simple practice can help activate your body's relaxation response and counteract the effects of stress. Additionally, make time for physical activity, aim for at least 30 minutes a day of moderate exercise, whether it's walking, jogging, swimming, or any other activity you enjoy. Exercise releases endorphins, which can improve mood and alleviate stress. Beyond managing stress, it is crucial to maintain both physical and mental health through healthy habits. Eat a balanced diet, rich in fruits, vegetables, whole grains, lean proteins, and healthy fats. Avoid processed foods, sugary snacks, and excessive caffeine consumption. These dietary choices can have a profound impact on your overall well-being. Sleep is another critical component of a healthy lifestyle, aim for at least 7-8 hours of sleep each night, creating a consistent bedtime routine to signal to your body that it's time to rest. Poor sleep can lead to decreased cognitive function, irritability, and a weakened immune system. Finally, do not hesitate to seek medical attention when experiencing symptoms of illness. Ignoring health concerns can exacerbate existing problems and create new ones, further hindering your work-life balance and personal well-being.

Imagine once more that tranquil lake, by managing stress and maintaining healthy habits, you can preserve the stillness of its surface and the peacefulness of your mind. In doing so, you will be better equipped to navigate the tightrope of work-life balance and prioritize your personal well-being in the pursuit of success.

Picture a vibrant garden, teeming with life and color, the roots of each plant are intertwined, supporting one another as they grow. This garden represents your personal relationships, the essential network that sustains you in both your professional and personal life. Maintaining these relationships requires time and effort. Family, friends, and colleagues all contribute to your overall well-being, providing emotional support, advice, and camaraderie.

Consider scheduling regular date nights with your partner, this not only strengthens your bond but also allows you to unwind from the stressors of work. I recall the last movie night I shared with my own spouse, how the laughter we shared had washed away the fatigue of a long week. Make it a priority to have lunch with a friend once a week. These moments of connection can be invaluable, giving you an opportunity to share triumphs and tribulations alike. I remember a recent lunch with an old college friend, the warmth of our conversation carrying me through the following days. Moreover, do not forget your colleagues, they too contribute to your overall well-being. Organize team-building activities or simply find time to engage in genuine conversations. These connections can foster empathy and understanding in the workplace, making it easier to navigate challenges together. Of course, nurturing relationships is but one aspect of prioritizing personal well-being, setting boundaries is equally crucial. For example, establish a time after which you will no longer check work emails. This allows you to fully disengage from work-related concerns, creating space for relaxation and rejuvenation. I reflect on my own routine, the peace I found in disconnecting from my inbox each evening. Delegating tasks to others can also create a healthier balance, recognize that you cannot – nor should you attempt to – shoulder the entire burden alone. By sharing responsibilities, you prevent burnout and make room for self-care." As I wrote these words, I acknowledged the relief I felt when entrusting certain tasks to my capable team members. Lastly, do not be afraid to take a mental health day when needed. Listen to your body and mind, recognizing when it is time to step back and recharge." I recalled a day I had spent in nature, the rejuvenating power of fresh air and sunlight working its magic on my weary soul. Returning to our garden metaphor, imagine the vibrant blooms and lush foliage that result from nurturing each plant. By cultivating your personal relationships and prioritizing your well-being, you too can flourish, achieving success while maintaining a healthy work-life balance.

For every well-tended garden, there are weeds that threaten to choke its growth. Consider the persistent demands of modern life – deadlines, meetings, commitments. How can one navigate this labyrinth and emerge unscathed, their well-being intact? Firstly, utilize a planner to schedule tasks and activities. By creating a clear roadmap for your time, you can better allocate it to both work and self-care. This simple tool has been invaluable in my own journey, allowing me to visualize and prioritize my commitments. Secondly, prioritize self-care activities. Recognize the necessity of nurturing your body, mind, and spirit. Carve out time for these pursuits, treating them with equal importance as your professional responsibilities. Lastly, learn to say no to non-essential tasks. Do not be afraid to decline invitations or requests that may detract from your well-being. In doing so, you create space for what truly matters. I remember a time when I chose to forgo a social event in favor of spending quality time with my family, a decision that ultimately fostered a deeper connection with my loved ones.

Yet we must also confront the consequences of neglecting personal well-being. Allow me to share some real-life examples of individuals who have experienced these consequences. Consider the story of a once-thriving entrepreneur, driven by ambition and determination.

Regrettably, she sacrificed her well-being in pursuit of success, ultimately succumbing to burnout. Her eventual emotional and physical exhaustion that led to a collapse of both her business and personal relationships. Or ponder the tale of a talented artist, plagued by anxiety and depression as a result of neglecting his own self-care. His inability to create due to the crushing weight of his emotions – a direct consequence of ignoring his personal well-being. Let these stories serve as cautionary tales. In the quest for success, do not lose sight of the importance of maintaining a healthy work-life balance and prioritizing your personal well-being. For without it, even the most beautiful gardens may wither and die.

However, amidst the cautionary tales, there also exist inspiring stories of those who have achieved a harmonious work-life balance and reaped the benefits of personal well-being. Let us now turn our attention to these paragons of success. Firstly, consider the life of a high-powered executive, seemingly bound to an existence dictated by the clock and the demands of her clients. But this extraordinary woman learned to prioritize her own well-being, and in doing so, discovered an inner strength that allowed her to manage her time more effectively. Every morning, she would rise before the sun, dedicating thirty minutes to meditation and deep breathing exercises, followed by a nutritious breakfast. She ensured that her weekends were reserved exclusively for quality time spent with family and friends, nurturing the relationships that mattered most to her. By prioritizing her well-being, this remarkable individual experienced increased happiness, improved relationships, and better overall health – tangible results supported by numerous research studies and statistics.

Take a study conducted by renowned psychologists Lyubomirsky, King, and Diener, which found that happier individuals are more likely to achieve success across multiple life domains, including work performance, social relationships, and physical health. Another example worth noting is the research of Dr. Michael Marmot, which highlights the correlation between social relationships and longevity. According to his findings, individuals with strong social connections tend to live longer, healthier lives compared to those who are isolated. Thus, it becomes clear that the path to success is not paved with relentless ambition alone, but rather with a healthy balance between work, personal well-being, and nurturing the relationships that truly matter. This is not a mere suggestion, but a fundamental truth, backed by science and exemplified by the lives of those who have achieved greatness while maintaining their inner harmony.

Let us now journey together toward putting this wisdom into practice. The road to success encompasses a delicate balance of professional ambition and personal well-being, as we have explored thus far. It is time for you to take action and prioritize the elements that make up a fulfilling life. Begin by devising your own self-care plan, tailored to your unique needs and circumstances. Consider the various facets of your life, including physical health, mental wellness, emotional growth, and social connections. Once you have identified the areas in which you wish to invest energy and care, set achievable goals for both work and personal life. For instance, you may commit to taking three 10-minute breaks throughout your workday for deep breathing exercises or dedicating one evening each week to nurturing your friendships. Stay true to these intentions, as they are the stepping stones that will lead you to the harmonious existence so many strive for yet seldom attain. Moreover, remember that the pursuit of success and happiness is not a solitary endeavor. Surround yourself with like-minded individuals who also value their own well-being and make it their mission to support one another in achieving balance. Empower yourself to forge ahead, knowing that you are not alone in your quest for fulfillment, and that countless others walk this path alongside you, all seeking to achieve work-life balance and success while maintaining good health and relationships.

Let me summarize the key takeaways from our exploration: Prioritize your personal well-being as a fundamental component of achieving success; create a personalized self-care plan that addresses your unique needs; establish achievable goals for both work and personal life; and seek the support of those who share your values and aspirations.

Go forth and create a life that is rich in both professional achievement and personal fulfillment. For it is along this path that one may find true happiness, balance, and ultimately, a life well-lived.

Lifelong Learning and Continuous Improvement

To illustrate the importance of acquiring new skills in achieving success, consider the story of Thomas Edison, a man whose insatiable appetite for learning fueled his invention of the light bulb and countless other groundbreaking technologies. He once famously said, I have not failed. I've just found 10,000 ways that won't work. This relentless pursuit of knowledge allowed him to hone his problem-solving abilities and ultimately achieve extraordinary success. Similarly, organizations such as Apple have thrived by fostering a culture of innovation, driven by a commitment to staying ahead of the curve. By continually pushing the boundaries of technology, design, and customer experience, they have redefined industry standards and disrupted established markets. Imagine, a world where each of us embraces the challenge of lifelong learning and seeks to continually improve ourselves. The potential for growth, both personally and professionally, would be limitless. Yet, all too often, we become complacent in our abilities, content to rest on our laurels rather than strive for greater heights. This is not only detrimental to our own development but also stifles progress and innovation on a broader scale. Remember, that success is not a static state, but an ongoing process of growth and adaptation. Seek out new opportunities to learn, expand your horizons, and unlock the untapped potential that lies within you.

Listen closely, for I am about to reveal the benefits that come from acquiring new skills and engaging in lifelong learning. Take, for example, the story of Alice a talented software engineer who found herself at a crossroads in her career. Seeking growth and new challenges, she decided to invest her time in learning a new programming language. As she immersed herself in this new skill, not only did she find herself more confident in her abilities, but she also discovered innovative ways to approach problem-solving within her own projects. Or consider the case of Jack, a seasoned marketing professional who took it upon himself to learn about emerging trends in social media advertising. Thanks to his newfound understanding, he was able to develop highly effective campaigns that resulted in increased sales and job opportunities. Indeed, the pursuit of new skills can unlock doors you never even knew existed.

Ah, but how does one embark on this journey of continuous learning? you might wonder. Fear not, for I have just the advice you seek. Begin by seeking out conferences and seminars relevant to your field. Such gatherings are a treasure trove of insights, offering opportunities to network with like-minded professionals while staying up-to-date with industry trends. Next, explore the vast expanse of online courses. Platforms such as Coursera, Udemy, and LinkedIn Learning offer a plethora of resources to expand your skillset, and many are available at little or no cost. Of course, don't overlook the power of industry publications, subscribing to relevant journals, magazines, or newsletters can provide valuable insights into emerging trends and best practices. Finally, seek out mentorship opportunities, whether through formal programs or informal connections, learning from those who have walked the path you now tread can prove invaluable in your own journey.

Remember, the pursuit of knowledge is an adventure that knows no bounds. Embrace it with open arms, and let it guide you towards success and fulfillment in both your personal and professional life.

Let's explore the importance of continuous improvement in maintaining success. Staying adaptable and open to change is the key to staying ahead of the competition.

Consider the story of a small business owner named Sarah. She owned a brick-and-mortar store selling handmade soap and bath products. When the pandemic struck, she swiftly adapted her business model by pivoting to e-commerce, allowing her to continue serving her customers in a safe and convenient manner. This willingness to embrace change not only saved her business but opened up new avenues for growth and expansion. Another compelling example is that of a software engineer named David. In the ever-evolving world of technology, David made it his mission to stay abreast of industry advancements. He continuously dedicated time to learning new programming languages, attending workshops, and collaborating with fellow engineers. As a result, he became an invaluable asset to his company, helping them stay ahead of competitors and develop cutting-edge solutions. Both Sarah and David, demonstrate the power of adaptability and continuous improvement in their respective fields. Adaptability allows individuals and organizations to respond effectively to changes in the market or industry. By staying agile and embracing innovation, they can capitalize on emerging opportunities before their competitors do. Take, for instance, the case of a major car manufacturer that quickly recognized the potential of electric vehicles and invested heavily in research and development. By staying attuned to industry trends and embracing change, they were able to get a head start on their competition and become a leader in the electric vehicle market. Likewise, consider a marketing agency that transitioned from traditional advertising methods to a data-driven, digital-first approach. By staying ahead of the curve and continuously honing their skills, this agency was able to provide their clients with unparalleled insights and results, thus outperforming their competitors.

Each of these examples illustrates the immense power of adaptability and continuous improvement in achieving success and staying ahead in an ever-changing world.

Allow me to share with you some invaluable resources that can help you on your journey toward such a world. By seeking feedback from mentors, colleagues, or even yourself, you create a vital channel for growth. Embrace this feedback with an open mind and heart, for it will be the compass that guides you through the uncharted waters of personal and professional development. Furthermore, the practice of setting goals and tracking progress will serve as both motivation and barometer for your journey. Break down your aspirations into manageable steps and celebrate each milestone, however small, knowing that they are propelling you ever forward. Take inspiration from the many successful individuals and organizations who have embraced lifelong learning and continuous improvement as cornerstones of their success. Consider, for instance, the renowned cellist who, despite achieving immense acclaim, still devotes hours each day to honing her craft, never content to rest on her laurels. Or the software company that has made a commitment to ongoing employee education, investing not only in the latest technologies but also fostering a culture of intellectual curiosity and collaboration. By prioritizing the development of their team members, this organization has positioned itself at the forefront of innovation, continually outpacing its competitors. Dear reader, emulate these luminaries by integrating the practices of feedback, goal-setting, and progress tracking into your daily life. For it is through such diligence and dedication that you, too, can join the ranks of those who have achieved success through lifelong learning and continuous improvement."

But we must not be naive to the challenges that may arise in the pursuit of lifelong learning and continuous improvement. For instance, in the whirlwind of modern existence, finding the hours to devote to new skills or staying abreast of industry trends can feel like an insurmountable task. Moreover, the sheer volume of information at our fingertips can be overwhelming, leading to paralysis by analysis or the dreaded imposter syndrome. Yet fear not for there are strategies to surmount these challenges, ensuring you stay on the path to success. First, break down your goals into smaller, achievable steps. Focus not on the daunting enormity of your objective, but rather on the incremental progress that will lead you there. Second, seek out an accountability partner – someone who shares your aspirations and is willing to support you through the journey. Finally, establish a routine and set aside dedicated time for learning and skill development. Treat it as an appointment with yourself – a sacred commitment to your growth. By employing these strategies, you can overcome the obstacles that stand between you and your dreams, forging onward in the quest for knowledge and self-improvement."

With the challenges and solutions laid out before you, dear reader, I now beseech you to take the plunge into the swirling waters of lifelong learning. Your path forward may appear daunting, yet it remains a journey worth embarking upon. "Will you accept my challenge? Will you strive for growth with every breath, stepping boldly into the unknown?" Start by making small commitments. Set aside a few minutes each day to delve into an article or watch an instructional video. Then, gradually increase your investment in yourself, as a gardener would nurture their tender sapling. Join me in attending conferences and workshops, engaging in spirited discussions with colleagues and mentors, and subscribing to industry publications to stay abreast of the latest trends. Remember that the first step is often the hardest. Yet, once your foot is firmly planted on the path, the journey becomes more manageable, even exhilarating. Consider the accomplishments of those who have come before us. They too faced trials and tribulations, but through dedication and perseverance, they triumphed over adversity, shaping our world in the process.

Paying It Forward and Giving Back

Picture this: A young child, eyes wide with excitement as they receive a gift from a complete stranger. The gift is not extravagant, but it is life-changing. The child's family beams with gratitude, knowing that this small act of kindness will set them on the path to a brighter future. This is just one example of the power of paying it forward and giving back to the community. Remember there's no such thing as a small act of kindness. Every act creates a ripple with no logical end – Scott Adams. When we give back to our community, we are not only helping others on their journey towards self-improvement and financial prosperity but also enriching our own lives in immeasurable ways. Before we delve deeper into the benefits of philanthropy and volunteer work, let us define two key terms that will guide our understanding of this topic: "self-improvement" and "financial prosperity." "Self-improvement" refers to the conscious efforts individuals make to better themselves in various aspects of their lives, be it physically, mentally, emotionally, or spiritually. It is an ongoing process where one constantly seeks to acquire new knowledge, skills, and experiences to grow as a person and reach their full potential. "Financial prosperity" is a state of economic well-being characterized by a continuous flow of income, savings, and investments. It involves having enough monetary resources to cover one's basic needs, secure financial stability for themselves and their families, and achieve long-term financial goals.

The practice of philanthropy and volunteer work is about more than just providing material support or temporary relief to those in need. It is about empowering individuals, families, and communities to overcome challenges and obstacles, enabling them to achieve their goals and ultimately, improve their quality of life. As you embark on this journey of giving back to your community, remember that the benefits are not just limited to those who receive your help. Your own personal growth and financial prosperity can also be enhanced by these acts of kindness.

"Give, and you shall receive" is a saying that holds true for philanthropy and volunteer work. By sharing your time, skills, and resources with others, you are not only making a positive impact on their lives but also enriching your own experiences and expanding your horizons. As we move forward through this book, let us keep in mind the importance of giving back to our communities and helping others on their paths to self-improvement and financial prosperity. Embrace the power of paying it forward and witness the incredible ripple effect it can create in the world around you.

To better understand the profound impact of giving back, let us examine the lives of individuals who have used their success to inspire and support others. These stories not only illustrate the power of philanthropy and volunteer work but also demonstrate how these acts can change lives and create lasting change. Consider the story of Oprah Winfrey, a media mogul and philanthropist who has dedicated her life to helping others. Born into poverty, she overcame numerous obstacles to become one of the most influential women in the world. Through her various platforms, she has been able to inspire millions by sharing stories of triumph and perseverance. "Success is meaningless," Oprah once said, "if you can't use it to lift someone else up." She took this philosophy to heart when she founded the Oprah

Winfrey Foundation, which aims to improve access to education and empower women across the globe. Oprah's generosity and commitment to giving back has had a far-reaching impact on countless lives, as evidenced by the thousands of students who have benefited from her foundation's scholarships and programs. Another inspiring figure is John, a small business owner who decided to make a difference in his community after achieving financial prosperity. Growing up in a low-income neighborhood, he was acutely aware of the challenges faced by many of its residents.

"Growing up, I saw firsthand the struggles people in my community faced every day," John shared during a recent interview. "When I became successful, I knew I wanted to use my resources to help those who are still struggling." John began by volunteering at a local food bank, donating both his time and money to ensure that families in need could put food on the table. As his business continued to grow, so did his philanthropic efforts. Today, John provides financial support to a number of local nonprofit organizations focused on education, healthcare, and economic empowerment. These two examples showcase the transformative power of giving back. Oprah Winfrey and John, despite coming from vastly different backgrounds, have both managed to overcome hardships and achieve their goals. Their stories also illustrate the incredible impact that philanthropy and volunteer work can have on both the giver and the receiver.

"Success is not just about what you accomplish in your life," Oprah once said. "It's about what you inspire others to do." In the spirit of these words, may we all find ways to lift others up and create a positive ripple effect that extends far beyond our own lives.

The transformative power of giving back is a force that cannot be understated. Imagine, for a moment, the image of a young boy, his face lit up with joy as he receives a new pair of shoes to replace the tattered ones on his feet. At the same time, picture the volunteer who handed him those shoes, her heart swelling with pride and fulfillment for having made a difference in this child's life. This scene, one that plays out countless times across the world, illustrates the incredible benefits of philanthropy and volunteer work for both the giver and the receiver. "Remember that the happiest people are not those getting more, but those giving more." These wise words by H. Jackson Brown Jr. encapsulate the essence of why giving back is so essential to our individual and collective well-being. It is in these moments of selflessness that we become enriched and transformed, discovering a sense of purpose and connection beyond our own lives. For the giver, engaging in philanthropy and volunteer work provides a multitude of benefits. Studies have shown that volunteering can lead to improved mental health and increased happiness, as it triggers the release of endorphins and promotes feelings of self-worth and accomplishment. Furthermore, the act of giving allows us to develop empathy and compassion, qualities that contribute to our overall emotional intelligence and interpersonal relationships. But the impact does not stop there. For the receiver, the benefits of philanthropy and volunteer work are just as profound. They receive not only the tangible goods or services being provided, but also the knowledge that someone cares about their well-being. This simple yet powerful message can instill hope and inspire motivation, ultimately empowering individuals to overcome challenges and pursue their own paths to self-improvement and financial prosperity.

Yet, the importance of giving back extends beyond the immediate exchange between giver and receiver. When we invest our time, energy, and resources into helping others, we foster a spirit of compassion and cooperation within our communities. This sense of unity and collective responsibility creates a positive impact on society as a whole, as we work together to address issues such as poverty, inequality, and injustice.

"Alone we can do so little; together we can do so much," said Helen Keller, a woman who understood the power of community support in overcoming adversity. It is with this sentiment that we must approach our efforts to give back. By recognizing the interconnectivity of our lives and embracing the notion that every act of kindness, no matter how small, has the potential to create lasting change, we can begin to build a brighter future for ourselves and those around us.

To further reinforce the significance of giving back to the community, let us delve into the world of statistics and research. Did you know that volunteering can lead to a 27% higher chance of finding employment after being out of work? This striking figure comes from a study conducted by the Corporation for National and Community Service in the United States. Furthermore, a study published in BMC Public Health found that individuals who volunteered regularly experienced reduced rates of depression and increased overall life satisfaction. "Numbers have an important story to tell. They rely on you to give them a voice," remarked Stephen Few, a prominent data visualization expert. With these numbers echoing in our minds, let us not merely see them as abstract figures but as tokens of hope and encouragement, urging us to take action and make a difference in our communities. "Kindness is the language which the deaf can hear and the blind can see," wrote Mark Twain. It is this universal language that we must embrace with open hearts, allowing it to guide our actions and shape our lives. For every act of giving back has the power to ripple through the fabric of society, creating waves of goodwill, compassion, and empathy.

But what does it mean to truly give back? How can we ensure that our efforts are met with lasting change? The answer lies within ourselves. We must first recognize our own strengths and abilities, utilizing them to create opportunities for others to thrive. In turn, we will find that our own lives become enriched, as we gain a deeper understanding of the interconnected nature of our world. "Thousands of candles can be lighted from a single candle, and the life of the candle will not be shortened. Happiness never decreases by being shared," said Buddha. With this wisdom as our guiding light, let us strive to illuminate every corner of our communities – sharing our gifts and talents, offering support and solace, and weaving threads of compassion that bind us all together.

Knowing that you have the power to positively impact the lives of others can be both an exhilarating and daunting realization. As you stand at the precipice of change, poised to take flight on the wings of compassion and generosity, I invite you to look within yourself and consider the myriad ways in which you might contribute to your community and help those around you on their respective paths towards self-improvement and financial prosperity.

Helping others is not just about money. It's about using the skills and resources we possess to make a difference. "Where do I begin?" you may ask, your eyes scanning the horizon for some sign or guidance. Fear not for I have compiled a list of practical tips and resources designed to assist you in your quest to give back:

1. Discover your passions: Reflect upon the issues and causes that are close to your heart, and seek out organizations that align with your values and interests.

2. Share your skills: Offer your expertise – whether it be in the realms of business, education, technology, or the arts – to nonprofits in need of guidance and support.

3. Volunteer your time: Lend a helping hand at local food banks, shelters, schools, or hospitals, providing invaluable service to those who need it most.

4. Make a monetary contribution: If your financial situation allows, consider making a donation to an organization that supports the cause you're passionate about.

5. Connect with others: Forge relationships with like-minded individuals, pooling your collective resources and working together to enact change.

So, I encourage you to embrace this call to action with open arms, and embark upon your journey towards philanthropy and volunteer work. In doing so, you will not only help those in need, but also foster your own personal growth and development, becoming a beacon of hope and inspiration for others to follow. Let us rise together and create a world where everyone has the opportunity to achieve self-improvement and financial prosperity. And with each step that you take, know that you are contributing to the tapestry of a brighter, more compassionate future for all.

To truly understand the transformative power of giving back, let us delve into the lives of those who have made a difference in their communities through their philanthropic efforts. Feel the warmth and pride that emanates from their stories, as you, dear reader, prepare to embark on your own path of change. Consider Sarah, a successful entrepreneur who built her fortune from scratch. She could have easily retired early, basking in the glow of her accomplishments. Yet, she chose to invest her wealth and time into a foundation dedicated to providing education and support for underprivileged children. The smiles on the faces of these young learners, as they grasped opportunities previously out of reach, lit up Sarah's life with purpose and fulfillment.

"Every child deserves a chance," Sarah had said, her voice resolute, "and I am committed to making that happen, one step at a time." Or reflect upon John, a renowned surgeon known for his skilled hands and compassionate heart. Though he could have opted for a lucrative private practice, he chose to spend his weekends volunteering at free clinics, offering life-changing medical care to those who could not afford it otherwise.

"Healthcare is a right, not a privilege," John asserted, his eyes brimming with conviction. "I believe my skills are meant to be shared with those who need them most." As you read their stories, feel the stirrings of inspiration within your soul, beckoning you to join this noble cause. For every individual who chooses to give back, countless lives are touched, and the seeds of hope and prosperity are sown –

not just for the beneficiaries, but also for the givers themselves.

"Where do I begin?" you asked yourself, determined to make a difference. The answer, my dear reader, lies within the following practical advice: First, identify your passions and strengths. Are you skilled in teaching? Do you have a penchant for helping the elderly or providing companionship to those who are lonely? By aligning your efforts with your talents, you maximize the impact you can make in your community. Next, research local organizations and initiatives that could benefit from your unique skills. Reach out to friends, family members, or neighbors who may have connections or insight into these groups. Remember, networking is a powerful way to discover opportunities to give back. Once you've found an organization that resonates with your passions and goals, commit to a schedule that fits your lifestyle. Start small, maybe just a few hours a week – consistency is key, and even the smallest acts of kindness can create significant change over time. As you venture into the world of philanthropy and volunteerism, remember to stay open to learning and growing. Embrace new experiences, listen to the stories of others, and allow yourself to be transformed by the journey. Finally, never underestimate the power of sharing your experiences with others. By inspiring those around you to join in your efforts, you amplify the positive impact on your community.

Final Thoughts and Ongoing Support

As we come to the final chapter of "Mastering the Grind: The Path to Self-Improvement and Financial Prosperity," I want you to take a deep breath and imagine yourself standing on the edge of a precipice, gazing out at the vast expanse before you. This landscape represents your future, filled with infinite opportunities for growth, success, and fulfillment. You've made it this far, dear reader, by working hard, remaining dedicated, and committing yourself to continuous learning. With every step you take, you'll forge an unbreakable bond between self-improvement and financial success. "Mastering the Grind" began as a seedling, a humble idea that grew into a sturdy tree brimming with knowledge and insight. It has been my pleasure to guide you through the dense forest of personal development and watch as you cultivated the necessary skills and habits to thrive in today's world. Allow me to remind you of the key themes and messages we've explored throughout our journey together:

First, the act of setting goals is paramount. Like a compass guiding a ship through stormy seas, clear and well-defined objectives will steer you towards your desired destination. By knowing precisely what you wish to achieve, you can plot a course, make adjustments along the way, and celebrate each landmark reached.

"Without goals, and plans to reach them, you are like a ship that has set sail with no destination." - Fitzhugh Dodson

Second, good habits are the building blocks of success. As Aristotle once said, "We are what we repeatedly do.

Excellence, then, is not an act, but a habit." Cultivate habits that propel you forward, such as waking up early, maintaining a healthy lifestyle, and investing time in learning new skills. These seemingly small actions, when performed consistently, compound over time and yield extraordinary results.

"Successful people do what unsuccessful people are not willing to do. Don't wish it were easier; wish you were better." - Jim Rohn

Lastly, taking action is the catalyst that sets your dreams in motion. It's not enough to simply have a plan or develop good habits—you must act upon them. The world belongs to those who seize opportunities and take calculated risks. You cannot expect success to be handed to you on a silver platter; it must be earned through relentless determination and unwavering perseverance.

"Action is the foundational key to all success." - Pablo Picasso

In conclusion, I want to congratulate you for having the courage to embark on this transformative journey. Now, armed with these valuable insights, you are prepared to face the challenges that lie ahead. Remember, my friend, that hard work, dedication, and continuous learning are the ingredients necessary to achieve self-improvement and financial success. Your future is now within reach—grasp it, and never let go.

"Success is not final, failure is not fatal: it is the courage to continue that counts." - Winston Churchill

As you embark on your unique journey towards self-improvement and financial prosperity, remember that the path may be filled with challenges and setbacks. But do not let these obstacles deter you or weaken your resolve. Instead, view them as opportunities to grow stronger and wiser, for it is through overcoming adversity that true progress is made.

"Strength does not come from winning. Your struggles develop your strengths. When you go through hardships and decide not to surrender, that is strength." - Arnold Schwarzenegger

I understand that this journey can be daunting at times, and you may feel overwhelmed or uncertain about how to proceed. Rest assured, you are not alone in these feelings. The key is to trust in yourself, believe in your abilities, and remain steadfast in your pursuit of success. Each step you take, no matter how small, brings you closer to your ultimate goals.

"Believe you can and you're halfway there." - Theodore Roosevelt

To further support you on this life-changing journey, numerous resources and platforms are available to provide ongoing guidance and encouragement. For instance, online communities such as Reddit's r/selfimprovement and r/personalfinance offer invaluable advice and camaraderie from like-minded individuals who share your aspirations. Additionally, social media platforms like LinkedIn and Twitter host countless influencers and thought leaders who regularly share their expertise and insights on self-improvement and financial success.

For more personalized guidance, consider enrolling in coaching programs or workshops tailored to your specific needs. Websites like Skillshare and Udemy offer a vast array of courses designed to help you hone your skills and develop new ones, while renowned coaches such as Tony Robbins and Ramit Sethi provide comprehensive programs aimed at fostering personal growth and wealth-building.

"An investment in knowledge pays the best interest." - Benjamin Franklin

Remember, the resources mentioned here are merely a starting point; there is a wealth of knowledge and support waiting to be discovered. It is up to you to seek them out and utilize them to their fullest potential.

"Education is the passport to the future, for tomorrow belongs to those who prepare for it today." - Malcolm X

As you embark on this journey, it is crucial to recognize that challenges and obstacles will inevitably arise. It is how you face them that will determine your ultimate success. Let us now address some common hurdles and offer actionable advice to help you conquer them.

1. Procrastination: One of the most significant barriers to progress is the tendency to put off tasks or avoid making decisions. To overcome procrastination, break your goals down into smaller, manageable tasks, and establish specific deadlines for their completion. Utilize tools like to-do lists and timers to keep yourself accountable and maintain momentum.

2. Fear of Failure: The fear of failure can paralyze even the most ambitious among us. The key to moving past this fear lies in reframing your mindset. Embrace failure as an

opportunity for growth and learning, rather than a reflection of your worth or abilities. Reflect on past setbacks and use them to inform your future actions, always seeking improvement.

"Failure is simply the opportunity to begin again, this time more intelligently." - Henry Ford

3. Lack of Focus: In today's fast-paced world, distractions are everywhere and maintaining focus can be challenging. To sharpen your concentration, minimize external distractions by creating a conducive environment for work or study. Practice mindfulness techniques, such as meditation or deep breathing exercises, to enhance your mental clarity and presence.

4. Impostor Syndrome: The sneaking suspicion that you are undeserving of success or that your accomplishments are the result of luck rather than skill is known as impostor syndrome. Overcoming this mindset requires self-awareness and a willingness to acknowledge and celebrate your achievements. Seek out supportive friends, mentors, or coaches who can provide objective feedback and encouragement when doubts arise.

"Act as if what you do makes a difference. It does." - William James

Remember, the path towards self-improvement and financial prosperity is not without its challenges. However, armed with the right tools, resources, and mindset, you are more than capable of overcoming any obstacle that stands in your way.

"Success is not the key to happiness. Happiness is the key to success. If you love what you are doing, you will be successful." - Albert Schweitzer

"Your time is limited, don't waste it living someone else's life." - Steve Jobs

As you embark on this incredible journey towards self-improvement and financial prosperity, always remember that the power to change your life lies within your own hands. Your dreams and aspirations are deserving of your utmost dedication and effort. In the words of the great Oprah Winfrey, "The biggest adventure you can take is to live the life of your dreams."

"Believe in yourself! Have faith in your abilities! Without a humble but reasonable confidence in your powers, you cannot be successful or happy." - Norman Vincent Peale

You are not alone on this path. There are countless others who have faced similar challenges and have emerged victorious, stronger and more successful than ever before. Listen to their stories; let their experiences fuel your determination and inspire you to keep pushing forward.

"Success is not final, failure is not fatal: It is the courage to continue that counts." - Winston Churchill

As you forge ahead on your journey, never underestimate the value of sheer persistence and resilience. These qualities are at the core of every success story and will be instrumental in your own triumphs. Remember the wise words of J.K. Rowling, who once said, "It is impossible to live without failing at something unless you live so cautiously that you might as well not have lived at all – in which case, you fail by default."

"Success is walking from failure to failure with no loss of enthusiasm." - Sir Winston Churchill

Take heart in knowing that even the most accomplished individuals have faced setbacks along their way to greatness. Embrace each obstacle as an opportunity for growth and learning, and remind yourself that true success is built on perseverance and unwavering commitment.

"Success is not built on success. It's built on failure. It's built on frustration. Sometimes it's built on catastrophe." - Sumner Redstone

As you continue on your journey towards self-improvement and financial prosperity, remember the importance of maintaining a positive mindset and surrounding yourself with supportive individuals who share your vision and goals. As Helen Keller once said, "Alone we can do so little; together we can do so much."

"Your success and happiness lie in you. Resolve to keep happy, and your joy and you shall form an invincible host against difficulties." - Helen Keller

With every step you take towards realizing your dreams, never forget that the most valuable lessons often come from the challenges we face. Embrace each challenge as an opportunity for growth, and always strive to learn from the experiences of those who have walked this path before you.

"Success is to be measured not so much by the position that one has reached in life, but by the obstacles which they have overcome." - Booker T. Washington

Now, as we part ways, it is essential to keep the momentum alive. Your call to action is this: Set a specific goal that you will work towards over the next 30 days. Whether it's increasing your income, improving your health, or cultivating stronger relationships, commit to taking daily action towards achieving this goal. Furthermore, consider joining an online community or local group centered around personal development and financial success. These platforms offer invaluable support, resources, and connections that can propel you forward on your journey.

"Coming together is a beginning; keeping together is progress; working together is success." - Henry Ford

In closing, remember that the path to self-improvement and financial prosperity is not a straight line, nor is it devoid of obstacles. Embrace each challenge as an opportunity for growth and always strive to learn from those who have walked this path before you. With dedication, resilience, and the principles outlined in "Mastering the Grind" as your guide, there is no limit to what you can achieve.

"Believe in yourself! Have faith in your abilities! Without a humble but reasonable confidence in your own powers, you cannot be successful or happy." - Norman Vincent Peale

This journey will require unwavering commitment, the willingness to embrace new ideas, and the courage to face adversity head-on. But know that every step you take, every challenge you conquer, and every ounce of effort you pour into your endeavors will bring you closer to the life you've always envisioned. Remember, the greatest of achievements are often born from the humblest of beginnings.

"Success is not the key to happiness. Happiness is the key to success. If you love what you are doing, you will be successful." - Albert Schweitzer

And so, as we part ways at the conclusion of "Mastering the Grind" and you venture forth on your own personal odyssey, keep these words etched in your heart: You possess the power to transform your life. Every goal, every dream, every aspiration that burns within you can be realized through your own hard work, dedication, and unwavering belief in yourself.

Go forth, dear reader, and seize the wondrous opportunities that await. Forge your path to self-improvement and financial prosperity with every step you take, and let the knowledge contained within these pages serve as a compass guiding you towards success. And remember—you are not alone. Together, we will conquer our dreams and leave a legacy of greatness for generations to come.

"Whatever the mind of man can conceive and believe, it can achieve." - Napoleon Hill

Carpe diem—seize the day, my friends. Your journey begins now.

Max A.B. HEWITT

Table of Contents

- *For privacy reasons some names and stories may be slightly altered*